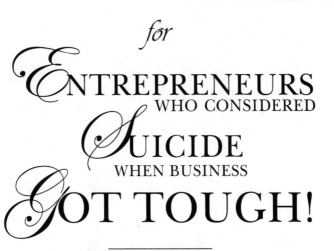

for

ENTREPRENEURS
WHO CONSIDERED
SUICIDE
WHEN BUSINESS
GOT TOUGH!

A Poetic Motivational
Business Manual

With more than 100 easy to apply
Survival Skills to help you succeed in business
plus...
A Directory of Funding Sources

DR. ROBERT S. SHUMAKE

GW Publishing
Detroit, MI

FOR ENTREPRENEURS WHO CONSIDERED
SUICIDE WHEN BUSINESS GOT TOUGH!

THIRD EDITION

© 2005 Robert S. Shumake
International Standard Book Number

978-0-977126-0-19

GW PublishingCo.
P.O. Box 241533
Detroit, MI 48224
email: GW Publishing Co@aol.com

Cover design and inside text design/layout by
Deborah L. Shumake, Designs by Ja`Phia. (313) 910-7957

Dedication

This book is dedicated to all the people who
have shared wisdom, knowledge, time,
and resources with me as I continue to
dream my dreams of reality.

Of course, I also dedicate this book to my
readers who I believe will find courage
within its pages as they continue their quest
for excellence in business.

and...
To my children, Jamelia, Diop, and Amina
who I believe will capture the
essence of doing business well.

C·O·N·T·E·N·T·S

C·O·N·T·E·N·T·S
Continued

Author's *Note*

NEWS FLASH!

The World Mourns the Suicide of a Dream at the Intersection of Hopeless Highway and Broke Boulevard

---

"It's a treacherous spot that every entrepreneur must pass on the way to Success Street," says the news anchorwoman on the Dream News Network. "Ironically, as often happens, this local John Dough took his tragic leap off the overpass just two blocks away from Don't Give Up Avenue."

The man's picture appears on the screen as the anchorwoman says: "According to our sources at Fate, this man was destined to become America's next great business tycoon. His invention would have revolutionized the way we live. But now, society must wait for someone with the perseverence and tenacity to triumph over the tragic defeat that murdered this man's aspirations."

Video flashes to a cemetery, then zooms in on a tombstone. The anchorwoman says, "While we should be reading John Dough's name on the Forbes 400 list, we now must focus on the inscription on his headstone. It says, "Herein lies a brilliant businessman who takes his God-

iii

given gifts to the grave because he allowed fear, frustration and financial worries to kill his dream before it was born."

Video shows the man giving a speech at a banquet; hundreds of people of every age and race rise to their feet, applauding the man's words. The anchorwoman says: "John Dough was well-respected and on his way to becoming a dynamic pioneer in the business world. And what makes this such a travesty, his family tells us, is that an international corporation called to make a major deal with him just hours after he plunged into oblivion."

The screen shows the man in a conference room; he's yelling at a dozen men and women who are shaking their heads. The anchorwoman says, "Like many of the three million entrepreneurs who have committed suicide, John Dough was depressed by failed business alliances and naysayers who criticized him for quitting his corporate job to pursue his dream."

The camera shows the anchorwoman, who says, "Now Fate tells us the man's spirit will be charged with Treason and First Degree Murder of a Dream."

This newsflash, in some form, has plagued the mind of every entrepreneur I know, including myself. God blesses us with a powerful gift, but too many of us never unwrap the gift to share it and make a positive difference in people's lives. Instead, we hide our gift, or drop it when the work seems too heavy to lift it up for display and celebration on the world stage.

The tragedy is that the world loses out on the power of great minds. What if Bill Gates had given up before inventing Microsoft Computers? What if John Johnson had found it too daunting to launch his pioneering media empire? What if Henry Ford had quit when his first engine failed? What if Thomas Edison had uttered, "Oh, what's the use!" before he made that first lightbulb glow?

The world might be in the dark, with no cars, computers or magazines. But these visionaries persevered past failure. In fact, I've read that the average millionaire fails 17 times before he or she succeeds.

That's why I wrote, *"For Entrepreneurs Who Considered Suicide When Business Got Tough."* Herein lie words to inspire you to focus and live your dreams. Remember what JC Penny said: you are always on the brink of bankruptcy or brilliance. So have faith that your brilliance will always outshine bankruptcy. You're at the Intersection of Success Street and Wealthy Way. Walk tall and jump at your dream!

Yes, for those who have heard that the curb on the sidewalk is as high as you can leap, this book is for you. For every start up business person afraid to take the ultimate challenge while knowing that the shackles of corporate America are enslaving them, this book is for you. To the small business owner who is trying to figure out how she is going to make payroll this month, don't quit; this book is for you.

"For Entrepreneurs Who Considered Suicide When Business Got Tough" has been written to inspire, motivate, assist and coach you in your mission of building your business. It is my desire that the notes, anecdotes, poems, and short narratives will uplift you during times when you are down, challenge you when you need that extra push, provide resources for your growth and help to monitor your mission. Most importantly, I hope that this book will be used as a daily prodder causing you to continue pressing forward to claim your personal victorious outcome.

This is a book for entrepreneurs. Whether you are just starting out, in the midst of daily operating your business or strategizing to build and grow your company into one of the world's greatest businesses, **For Entrepreneurs Who Considered Suicide When Business Got Tough!** has been designed for you. Go for it! Go On! **JUMP!**
Jump Into Success!
– This book is all for that!

Dr. Robert S. Shumake

PART ONE

PURPOSE

1

*"Always strive to be more than that which you are,
if you wish to obtain that which you are not."*
                                    – S.B. Fuller, Entrepreneur

*"A man without a purpose is like a mad dog
roaming the streets, chasing after
everything in sight."*
                                    – Robert S. Shumake

PURPOSE is knowing whose you are, who you are and what you are.

Knowing what you are born to do propels you to persist until the task is complete.

PURPOSE finds an open door among many closed doors.

PURPOSE conquers failure.

PURPOSE measures itself by purposeful ambitions rather than aimless accomplishments.

PURPOSE does not accept the labels of others.

PURPOSE defines itself through self-affirmation and steadfastness.

PURPOSE finds power and peace!

I call them "Aha! moments" — those brilliant epiphanies when something quite simple illustrates a profound fact about life as an entrepreneur. Well, an awesome "Aha! moment" happened during a grocery shopping trip-gone-wrong. I had decided to surprise my wife by preparing dinner. So I stopped by the store to buy bread, eggs, cheese, flour, vegetables and a few canned goods. I also picked up chicken breasts and olive oil. But catastrophe struck my gourmet meal as I loaded the groceries into the car. An ominous crunch sound let me know I was in for a challenge. Turns out, the cans had crushed the glass bottle of olive oil; my groceries glistened in a slippery slick in my trunk. At first, the mess symbolized those moments in business when everything is going according to plan, when **boom!** something explodes and drowns everything around it in chaos. But suddenly, the symbolism spun far deeper. As I began wiping the oil off the cans, cheese and veggies, an epiphany illuminated my thoughts. The thick, aromatic oil reminded me of a Sunday morning church service when our pastor explained the intricacies of transforming olives into a precious delicacy. He said that in order to produce one drop of olive oil, each tiny leaf of the olive tree is pressed separately to maintain its purity. The leaves are ground, crushed and put through a complicated process before the oil reaches our grocery carts. In Middle Eastern nations, the process of producing olive oil is often painstakingly slow. Hours, weeks, months and sometimes years go into ensuring that it is processed to perfection.

I realized, you can't rush perfection; pressing olive oil is a metaphor for the creation of an excellent entrepreneur. It takes many hours, days, weeks, months, and years to truly develop ourselves and our businesses into perfection. That idea takes on a spiritual depth because olive oil is an integral part of anointing in religious ceremonies. It is pure and worthy of such honor only because of what has gone into making it. It has withstood immense grinding and crushing to be used for its multiple purposes.

The same goes for us in business. Knowing our purpose enables us to submit to the process, knowing that it will produce superior products and services for our customers.

We often try to escape the grinding, but to grow, we must be pressed. The Pillsbury Dough Boy misquoted the wise men by stating, "Easy in, easy out." The real saying goes something like, "Hard in, holy out." Press yourself toward your purpose. You are ordained to do great business. Press on. And, keep pressing on so that you will experience an anointed, holy, miraculous outcome.

Knowing our purpose allows us the opportunity to be changed and expanded.

PART ONE: PURPOSE

❁

Create a Statement of Purpose for you and your business

❁

_____

_____

_____

_____

_____

_____

_____

_____

_____

_____

_____

_____

_____

_____

_____

_____

_____

_____

MISSION

"Every person is born into this world to do something unique and something distinctive. And if he or she does not do it, it will never be done."
— Benjamin E. Mays, Educator

"One's mission in life is determined by one's actions."
— Robert S. Shumake

The Mission is...
>   the will to press on long after others
>   have called you a failure.

The Mission is...
>   to identify accomplishment in your-
>   self when everyone around you
>   exudes negativity.

The Mission is...
>   to look up from the valley to see the
>   mountains.

The Mission is...
>   to continue dreaming when the
>   world tells you to be for real.

The Mission is...
>   to believe in the unseen; knowing
>   very well that insight has nothing to
>   do with eyesight.

The Mission is...
>   to know that the God who has cho-
>   sen you will keep His promises to
>   you.

The Mission is...
>   to finally realize that the only mistake
>   in life is in not having a mission.

My hamster used to amaze me as he'd run for hours on his little plastic wheel. Ben would sprint like there was no tomorrow; his dark little eyes looked intense as the pink pads of his feet raced like Fred Flintstone's bare feet that made his prehistoric car speed away. But Ben never got anywhere. He could run for his life, but he was stuck. So, after awhile, he'd tire himself out, crawl into a nest of woodchips, and fall asleep. Watching Ben do this day after day, sadly, reminded me of a lot of people.

Many people are literally running on the wheel of life, but they will never reach their destination. Every morning they hurriedly get up and sprint desperately to win the race of life. But too many folks don't even know where they're going. And a whole lot of others don't know how to get from Point A to Point B. So, like my pet hamster, they run in circles, tire out, and quit.

If you pay attention to the people who run in circles, you'll hear a chorus of vague, non-committal expressions such as: "One day I'm going to get my degree and open my business." Or they say, "When I get myself together, I'm gonna be the baddest entrepreneur in the city. But we don't believe their hype. Because they never take action beyond their false, grandiose promises to us and themselves. These folks need to watch Ben huffing and puffing in circles, day after day, year after year. That mirror image of their lives would make them see that they're stalling on a vicious cycle of mediocrity. Why?

11

Because they will not stop to reflect on their unique, individual mission in life. Only when one knows where one is going should one dash off to get there.

This reminds me of a friend who's always talking about a particular business he should start. He's forever telling me that he thinks it's the business for him. But he never takes action.

That's because he has failed to identify his own mission in life. And that leaves him without a clear and defined direction for doing what is required of a successful business man.

And how do we do that? First, go within. While I was watching Ben, I realized even his name has significance to this idea.

We have to know where we've "been" to understand where we are and where we can go. So if you don't already hear your calling, sit down, shut out the noise of the world, and focus on these questions: "What am I supposed to accomplish and contribute to the world during my lifetime? What gifts has God blessed me with? How can I package those gifts and present them to people who will benefit from them?"

For example, if you make mouth-watering red velvet cake, blueberry muffins and peach cobbler, you could consider opening a dessert business. Start small, in your kitchen; advertise and prosper! If you're a bodybuilder who knows martial arts and you love to protect people, perhaps a body guard business is your calling. If you love books, greeting cards and coffee, open a bookstore with a café—or a whole chain of them!

As you define your mission in life, ask your-self, "What am I passionate about? What do I love so much that I'd do it without getting paid? What skill do I have that can make people's lives better?"

This reminds me of one of my favorite quotes: "If you help enough people get where they're going, where you would like to go will surely follow."

You should always remember that your mission is not about dollars or prestige. It shouldn't be: "My mission is to own a company and make $20 million, then retire to Fiji." A true mission is altruistic; it's about doing something for the good of other people.

For the baker, it's about sweetening people's lives with baked treats. The bodyguard? Giving people that all-important feeling of being safe. The bookstore-café? Sharing knowledge and fellowship over coffee.

My mission, for example, is to raise enough scholarship money to give any, and everyone access to the cornerstone of success in life: an education. My childhood traumas of poverty and homelessness inspire this mission to enrich the minds of others so that poverty is never an obstacle to learning.

Search deep in your heart and soul to find your mission.

The answers you find will create a key to unlock a lifetime of happiness, prosperity and fulfillment for you. Your passion and purpose doing what you love will fuel your mission at turbospeed. You will never again be stuck on a wheel that's spinning fast and furiously but going nowhere. Instead, you'll be on a pleasure cruise atop the wheels of life as you speed happily toward your mission.

Develop a Mission Statement

_____

_____

_____

_____

_____

_____

_____

_____

_____

_____

_____

_____

_____

_____

_____

_____

_____

_____

_____

_____

A<small>TTITUDE</small>

"We all hope for the best, but an optimist expects to get it."

— *Montel Williams, Talk Show Host*

"Attitude shapes a person's thoughts, actions, and beliefs, and gives a person the choice to succeed or fail."

— *Robert S. Shumake*

A PERSON'S ATTITUDE CAN...
open doors or close them,
See beyond all obstacles or become
bound by them.

ATTITUDE CAN...
    win a game or lose it
    buoy your spirit or kill it
    keep you in the valley or
    place you on the mountain,
    strengthen your life or destroy it.

ATTITUDE has a way of finding the
good or bad in every situation,
guaranteeing the person either turmoil
or peace of mind.

PART ONE: PURPOSE

Apositive attitude saved my life.
Seriously, if I hadn't trained my strong
mind to overcome my weak body, I
would be dead right now.

Because from the moment I took my first
breath, asthma threatened to steal it from me.
I lived my first days on the precarious line between life and death — inside the harsh plastic
walls of an incubator. Then I spent weeks and
months, whole chunks of my childhood, in
the hospital. Asthma attacks didn't care if it
was Christmas or Thanksgiving. Little Robert
spent plenty of those special days hooked up to
oxygen and breathing treatments while the rest
of my family enjoyed turkey, presents and cozy
holidays at home.

I was sad and disappointed, and furious that
this disease was robbing me of those childhood
memories. But I never gave up.

Even as a small child, I understood that the
power of my mind could get my body through
anything. Even back then, I believed what pro-
athletes often say about enduring the grueling
challenges of a game: winning is 99% mental
but only 1% physical.

I smile now, because sometimes I was, as
kids are, a little hard-headed about it.

See, when I was about nine, a bigger boy on
our street in Detroit challenged me to a race. He
declared: "Robert, I'm gonna beat your butt!"
So I took off. I ran one block. And I won the
race!

19

But I ended up in the hospital that night, because exercise often causes asthma attacks. The next day, however, when I returned home, that kid challenged me again. This time, I ran two blocks. And I won! But again, I spent the night in the hospital.

When I came home the next night, I copped a positive attitude: if I can beat that bigger kid in a race, then I can overcome the asthma in my lungs. If you've ever had an asthma attack, you know that this is no easy feat. It feels like a giant fist is squeezing your chest, blocking all air passages. No air seems to be coming in or going out. I had it so bad, I even used to faint. But, I was determined to survive and win.

So the next night, when we raced, I ran for four blocks. And I kept running, and winning, with no asthma attacks! I cheered myself on with thoughts such as: "I'm a winner!" "You can do it!" "Failure is not an option!"

In fact, I got so good at healing my body with my mind, I set all the state regional track records for Edwin Denby High School; I continually set new meet records that still stand today. Even though I'd been a scrawny little kid who was always in the hospital, I became an All-City champ in track and field. That included the pole vault, the long jump, and the high and low hurdles.

Then I won a track scholarship to Ferris State University in northern Michigan. My record still stands as one of the top all-time track and field stars in the history of Ferris State University.

Back then, I still had asthma; in fact, it made me vomit during heats at track meets. But my positive attitude kept my feet pumping at record speeds. And I became the college conference champion.

All thanks to positive thinking!

The illness never went away, but I kept it in perspective. I never viewed it as a handicap. And I never sat around and moped, "Oh man, I got asthma, I can't do nothin'!" I realized early on, that I could promote the best Pity Party in town, but nobody would ever show up!

Instead, I share my stories, telling others that, "You can do it, too!"

That's how inspired I feel when I read about the man who invented those small logs that we use to light our fireplaces – Duralogs. This visionary suffered third degree burns in a fire. As a result, he was forced to use a wheelchair. But his tragedy was turned into a triumph that now warms millions of people and generates millions of dollars every year.

So how does one person keep a positive attitude, even in the midst of illness and tragic circumstances, while some folks constantly whine and complain about everything?

It's a daily decision. Today I can cop a positive attitude, or I can grumble and groan all day long. But guess what? Nobody wants to be around a complainer. Except those of likemind. Since misery loves company, it attracts negative people and experiences.

I guarantee, if you wake up tomorrow and say, "This is going to be a wonderful day," it will become a self-fulfilling prophecy.

I credit my parents for encouraging me to look for the good in people and situations. "Read this book," my father would say, handing over stacks of reading materials with positive messages. Dad introduced me to positive thinking gurus like Dennis Waitly and Wayne Dyer; they taught me positive affirmations that strengthened my mind and my body.

As an adult, I devour books. At one point, I had an $800-a-month book habit. I can't get enough of self-help books such as The Power of Positive Thinking by Norman Vincent Peale. Dr. Peale reinforces what I strongly believe: it is impossible to accomplish anything great while continuously operating with a negative attitude.

Just look around. Everything you see, taste, touch, hear and smell was either built, created, bought or developed by someone who had a positive attitude. They chose to take great risks to make their idea a concrete reality. Builders, visionaries and successful people know that a good attitude and a strong purpose can squash negative influences.

They also avoid negative people because

negativity is poisonous and contagious. Walk into a room with negative people and you'll see that they literally dim the lights of possibility.

Knowing this makes it imperative that you put your friends, family and colleagues on the Scale of Positive and Negative. If they're heavy with negative vibes, they're weighing you down. They'll shoot down your ideas. They will create maddening, time-draining dramas. And, they will also make you question yourself to the point that you think about pinning a suicide note to your dream and casting it into the Entrepreneurial Graveyard.

My advice? Run, fast, away from anybody with a negative attitude. Let no one's negativity weigh you down. Surround yourself with folks whose positive words and actions help you soar. If winning is 99% psychological, then a positive mind can only bring phenomenal success!

---❂---

Develop a Positive Attitude

---❂---

Find a positive quote, book, scripture or tape and use it daily.

_____

_____

_____

_____

_____

Determine the positive people in your life and stick to them like glue.

_____

_____

_____

_____

Quarantine yourself from all the negative people in your life... they are contagious.

_____

_____

_____

_____

DOING IT!

"Try not, Do or Do Not."
— Yoda, The Empire Strikes Back

"Action is the first key to success –
first in the mind, then in the physical world."
— Robert S. Shumake

We're all waiting for our ship to come in, but if you're filling the sails of your entrepreneurSHIP with wishes and not winds of focused vision, you'll be waiting forever.

Because success doesn't sail on wishes. It takes years of sweat equity, pumping those purpose driven oars, and generating strong winds of focused mission, to sail into the Port of Success.

That's the place where we find the financial rewards, the fulfillment and the recognition we deserve for setting sail with our dreams.

This precious cargo starts off as nothing but a fleeting, invisible thought. But with the solid strength of belief and a plan that maps our way across treacherous seas of uncertainty, failure, financial fears and human horrors, we can arrive safely through golden gates of opportunity.

Even with the best ideas and sharpest visions, we are navigating through both calm waters and stormy squalls. With the right plan mapping out the way, we'll come out stronger and better for it. But we must set sail with the belief that we have to sail out to success, not party at the marina and wait for success to wash up waves of cash, checks and accolades. No, to captain your EntrepreneurSHIP into your Promised Land of Success, you've got to keep rowing when your fingers are blistered. Have faith that a strong wind of opportunity will blow and fill your sails with prosperity. Find energy even when you want to collapse with fatigue. Stay your course by focusing on your destination. All that will get you there.

Because in the ebb and flow of business and life, sunshine and rainbows always follow even the most brutal hurricanes and tsunamis. So it's up to us to prepare our minds – our ships to weather the storms.

If your entrepreneurSHIP tosses you into a swirling abyss of failure and financial loss, don't be afraid to scream for someone to toss you a life ring or send in a rescue chopper. Help will come. You will survive. You'll learn how you fell off course. And you'll figure out an even better route.

Because success is not about how you chill on the deck of your entrepreneurSHIP with a cocktail. True success is measured by how quickly you can swim up and out of the abyss when you fall in. Then winds will be created to fill your sails and propel you into dreams-come-true. And where does that wind come from?

Faith. Hard work. And the Spirit. These energize your mind, heart, and soul. But, if your entrepreneurSHIP still doesn't budge, then:

Grit your teeth,

Feel the wheel,

Say another prayer,

Call on your mates,
Lean into your purpose,
Seek out your mission,
Check out your attitude,
And heave ho!
You will go.
You will make it happen.
You will earn it,
Talk it,
Walk it,
Do it!
And your ship will come in loaded with mind-blowing riches!

S avoring the satisfaction of your reaction when you seal a hot deal.

U plifting your gifting of the world with ambition and precision.

C reating a spirit, the world hears it, gets near it, endears it, cheers it!

C aressing your blessing not stressing just dressing with style and professing love.

E xecuting transmuting every detail with beauty.

S tanding tall and demanding that all unbelievers become achievers.

S eeking victory wild and free loving every step of a divine journey.

❖
List of Successes; Celebrate Them!
❖

_____

_____

_____

_____

_____

_____

_____

_____

_____

_____

_____

_____

_____

_____

_____

_____

_____

_____

_____

_____

TRUE FREEDOM

"Possession of material riches without inner peace is like dying of thirst while being in the river."
— Paramhansa Yogananda

"True freedom lives in a person's state of thinking."
— Robert S. Shumake

True Freedom

True Freedom
is more than marches,
pickett signs
and protests.

True Freedom holds more clout
than designer clothes,
fancy cars, homes and
large bank accounts.

True Freedom is not integration,
corporate positioning
or Sunday church visits.

True Freedom is the ability
to enjoy peace of mind,
and hear the echo of
Dr. Martin Luther King, Jr.:

"I'm Free At Last!
I'm Free At Last!
Thank God Almighty
I'm Free At Last!!!"

PART ONE: PURPOSE

Slavery was supposed to end back in 1863 when President Abraham Lincoln — "The Great Emancipator" of America — freed millions of slaves.

But even though the Emancipation Proclamation outlawed slavery, masses of people are still shackling their minds with mediocrity and inferiority.

This tragic mental enslavement is just as stifling and oppressing as the brutal, plantation-owning slave masters of the 1700s and 1800s. Instead of a man with a whip and the authority of ownership, these modern-day masters are such wickedly intangible forces as ignorace, poverty, fear and laziness.

They enslave the thoughts and actions of millions who, as a result, merely exist rather than live. Mediocrity smashes any hope for excellence. Low expectations are dead weight holding down aspirations.

This sad segment of America proves that saying: most people die at age 25, but wait until age 65 for their burial.

Because when a dream dies, it kills potential and happiness and hope. It leaves an empty hull of a human being who robotically goes through the motions of life, never savoring the joys of success.

In fact, watching folks whose minds are enslaved by fear and hopelessness is like watching the movie, "Night of the Zombies." And people who wallow in substandard lives with no desire to improve through education or employment cause me to think like the pistol-toting "Black Moses" — Harriet Tubman — would tell

33

the slaves: "Either you come with me, or you'll die here a slave."

Her mission in life was to lead people to freedom. Despite threats of murder, a bounty on her head for capture, and packs of dogs following her, Harriett continued her mission; she courageously guided people through fields and forests, lit only by the moon and the North Star to find a better life for themselves and their future generations.

It seems that too many folks today have no vision of tomorrow, let alone the next generation. It's all about forgetting the pathetic state of today by clubbing, drugging, cruising and surrendering to other frivolous pursuits. When one's mind is enslaved, coming up with a life mission is impossible.

That's why it's my mission in life to empower others to achieve mental and financial freedom as entrepreneurs. That starts with education; my scholarship fund is a sure-fire way to help people break free from their mental shackles and flee into a world of productivity and prosperity.

Education trains and encourages entrepreneurs as tireless freedom seekers. They, in turn, will use their minds and dreams to cultivate opportunities for others to escape mental, physical, and material chains; they do this by providing products and services for the benefit of humanity.

Freedom is a real change of consciousness for the good of self and the world. We should all draft an Emancipation Proclamation -- a plan to reach out to those whose minds are still shackled by mediocrity. We as entrepreneurs must share the infectious power of our passion to inspire folks to see another way, to follow our path to freedom. Here, we can let the joy of freedom ring in our products, services and relationships with customers.

Together, we can save lives through empowering others to pursue their dreams.

✿

Write A Business Emancipation

✿

What do you need to do to free yourself?

_____

_____

_____

_____

_____

_____

_____

_____

_____

_____

_____

_____

_____

_____

_____

_____

_____

_____

_____

SURVIVAL SKILLS
FOR
Purpose-
Driven
ENTREPRENEURS

Eight Entrepreneurial Survival Skills

1. ASSESS YOURSELF! Just because you know how to run a business, doesn't mean you know your product or service backward and forward. And vice versa. So critique yourself; find out your strengths and weaknesses. Then make everything your strengths.

2. LEARN BUSINESS SKILLS! You might have the hottest idea since the microwave oven, but if you have the business skills of a doorknob, your entrepreneurSHIP might spring a fatal leak. So become a business person; take a class or consult with a trusted mentor about how to run a company and how to create a powerful marketing plan. Let someone else develop the product; you can train them if necessary.

3. ASSEMBLE A DREAM TEAM! You'll need some experts to handle certain tasks. Hire a lawyer for all legal documents; the money you pay him or her will save you in legal fees down the road. Also, hire an accountant who will keep your money and your records organized. This will save your sanity, your financial status and many headaches if you're audited. And of course, hire good employees through referrals and thorough background checks.

4. PAY YOUR BILLS ON TIME! If you can't pay on time, call your supplier or other creditor before they call you to make arrangements. The arrangements should be definite with payment dates. Only make promises for payments that you plan to fulfill.

5. CASH DOESN'T BOUNCE! Never write bad checks or postdated checks. These undermine your credibility.

6. STUDY! Make learning and upgrading the motto for yourself and your staff. The expense of training your employees is worth it to your business output and professionalism.

7. SAY THANK YOU! Hold a "preferred customer preview" with advance invitations, simple refreshments, entertainment, and introductory price offerings applicable for the next 14 days. Allow your customers to bring guests. These should be the only new customers there. Customers will get a chance to testify about your business to their friends while having a great time.

8. SEEK REFERRALS! Referral- generated clients/customers normally spend more money, buy more often, and are more loyal and more friendly than any other type of business you might pursue. Referrals are the least expensive form of advertisement.

PART TWO

VISION

PERCEPTION

"A man's mind is the activating force that directs him. He does as he thinks"

> – Amy J. Garvey,
> wife of Marcus Garvey, philosopher

"Inner vision sees beyond and enters into perfect sight."

> – Robert S. Shumake

PERCEPTION

Perception is the way you look at something.
Is yours twenty-twenty, rich with plenty?
Or lack and losing, mad and confusing?

From a high-rise window, are folks on the
sidewalk a crowd of worthless ants?
Or opportunity?

In the ocean, do you see God's beautiful creation,
or are you angry that water went up your nose?

When crossing the finish line second,
Do you see that you lost the race;
or do you see the twelve people whom you were
in front of?

Do you see the number of times you failed at
something, or how many times you succeeded at
not repeating a mistake?

Your mind controls perceptions.
However you see a situation,
good or bad,
Just remember —
You are RIGHT!

A notorious gangster taught me the value of perception — how you see yourself, and how you allow otherse to view you. Even though this man was retired, word on the street still dubbed him as the most powerful, respected dude around.

When I asked him about his rise to the top of his underworld empire, he said rule number one was to "keep his fronts up."

In other words, this gangster's basic marketing tool was to make everybody believe he was larger-than-life. He dressed to the nines, he drove a stylish car, he flashed cash and flexed at every opportunity.

He in effect created a perception of himself as a big, bad gangster, and the world responded accordingly.

Was this bad or good? For him, it was good, because it made him effective at his business, however illegal it was. In the world of gangsters, he viewed himself -- and forced others to view him -- as a succcess.

And that's the moral of the story. Period.

If you want to be a successful entrepreneur, you have to endorse a perception of yourself that you are talented, deserving and capable of achieving any goal you set for yourself. Then it's your task to make everybody else believe that perception as well.

The possibilities are infinite.

Can Michael Jordan actually fly? The world sure believes he can. Is Coca-Cola really the best soft drink on the planet? Whether yes or no, its makers cultivated a marketing plan that ultimately made Coke the leading soft drink in the world.

Now think about your business.

What is the strength of the perception you have built in terms of integrity, quality, and service for your business? If it needs tweaking, and it probably does, strategize how to create a perception for your business that will catapult it to the top of your industry.

I had a moment of illumination at a recent conference on Mackinac Island in northern Michigan. My purpose there was to raise funds from some of the most powerful and wealthy people in America.

As I sat at the table with business tycoons such as Eugene Applebaum, founder of Walgreens, Tom Monaghan, founder of Domino's Pizza and gazillionaire who was building a yacht the length of a football field — I suddenly felt like an insignificant blip on the radar of the business world. I was an ant sitting amongst 800-pound gorillas. There I was, decades younger than these men, and the only African American at the table.

It was such a dizzying experience, I had to retreat to my room to regroup. I thought,"What am I doing here with these heavyweights?"

Then I realized, I ALREADY AM AN 800-POUND GORILLA! If I weren't, I wouldn't have been sent to that gathering with my important assignment.

The problem was, I had not until that point perceived myself as a king. I was suddenly aware that the powerhouse who sent me there had the faith that I could do an excellent job. He perceived me as an 800-pound gorilla who could handle this delicate task with the appropriate etiquette and confidence.

The lesson? I had to grow into my greatness. I had to accept and embrace the fact that yes, I already am a tycoon in my own right, and it's only a matter of time before I am as powerful as the other men who were sitting at the table.

It forced me to remember the awkward growing pains of adolescence. You remember that period, don't you? Your voice is changing, so when you try to talk to a girl, you squeak all over the English language, sounding anything but cool. You look down noticing that your feet had suddenly grown so big that you find you are stumbling over yourself.

Then, one day your grandmother complements you, remarking that you're looking handsome and tall and grown-up. All of a sudden, you begin to walk with a hip swagger. And you train your voice to speak in the deepest, coolest

Barry White baritone you can muster when talking to the girls.

Yes, it takes a while to self-actualize. Perhaps you will experience some very embarrassing, uncomfortable moments while stretching your vision, mission and goals from gawkiness to greatness.

But, it's all about what you believe. So remember, you are already an 800 pound gorilla. Believe it. Act like it. And remember to "keep your fronts up."

————— ✸ —————
Develop a Personal and Business Perception
————— ✸ —————

Solicit letters of en-
dorsement from re-
spected individuals,
politicians, clergy,
business people, and
organizations in
your community.

_____
_____
_____
_____
_____
_____

Create your own
powerstyle with
suits, shoes,
jewelry, etc.

_____
_____
_____
_____

Become more
knowledgable about
your industry than
your competitors.
Read. List and study
books and magazines
that pertain to your
business.

_____
_____
_____
_____

Increase your member-
ships in organizations;
make associations to
develop relationships
to help promote your
business's positive
perception.

_____
_____
_____
_____

WHAT A BLIND PERSON SEES...

---   ---

"I can see farther over the mountains than the man standing atop of it."

— *Gullah*

"One's inner vision is beyond the greatest depths of eyesight."

— *Robert S. Shumake*

---   ---

A BLIND MAN sees wealth through his heart, while a seeing man doesn't recognize any wealth that he can't see with his eyes.

A BLIND MAN sees the radiance of hope, while the seeing man views despair.

A BLIND MAN looks and finds peace, while a seeing man sees turmoil.

A BLIND MAN finds happiness within, while a seeing man looks for things to make him happy.

A BLIND MAN sees greatness within him, while a seeing man is blinded by his faults.

A BLIND MAN reaches his goals, while the seeing man keeps searching.

A BLIND MAN knows believing is seeing, while the seeing man only believes what he sees.

Simply, this BLIND MAN has...

The Power of Inner Vision.
Learn to see as the blind man!

Once I heard about the Ultimate Quam, I had to see it for myself. But I couldn't. In real life, that is.

In my mind, however, I envisioned it with all the spectacular glory that people had described to me.

See, The Ultimate Quam is something that most people never experience. In fact, most folks have probably never heard about it, and even if they do, they can't imagine it.

I became privvy to this phenomenon when I heard some wealthy men discussing the advantages of flying in a commercial aircraft versus flying one's own jet. One benefit of a private plane, they said, is the ability to fly higher. And with more height, they could get closer to the stars, providing them the chance to experience The Ultimate Quam — seeing the sky, the stars, and the earth meet!

At first I thought these men were pulling my leg. But listening to their descriptions of the euphoria of it, I decided, The Ultimate Quam had to be real.

So I began visualizing what it would be like to see the earth, the sky, and the stars meet. I wanted to see it for myself. I had to see it. I craved the chance to view the world from a completely different perspective. And that inspired me to ask: Can you visualize your life in a way that is wildly different from the life you know today? If you cannot, you must allow the blind man to teach you the power of inner vision.

It is a life-changing skill.

I realized that years after I'd heard about and imagined The Ultimate Quam.

I finally had the joy of experiencing it for myself. Believe me, it was exhilarating to see what my previous mind had deemed impossible — a meeting of the sky, the stars, and the earth!

But it was real!

This convinced me that the power of vision is what you make it. You can call things into existence, just as I had. Because, after years of visualizing myself on a private jet, experiencing The Ultimate Quam, my real life had placed me on a private plane that had a marble bathroom and a king-sized bed.

I realized that my inner vision had helped bring this incredible moment into being. But too often, we neglect our inner vision; some folks don't know how to see with it at all. But for our growth it's as necessary as the air we breathe.

It reminds me of the day my geography instructor asked us students, "Which is the largest nation?"

"Asia!" they called out. "Europe! Africa!"

The teacher agreed that those were indeed large nations.

"But the largest nation of them all," he said, "is the IMAGINATION!"

As an entrepreneur, your greatest gift to yourself is your ability to visualize what you want for your business.

Form a mental picture of yourself doing business with finesse and success. See with your mind's eye who will be your customers. Visualize the physical and financial growth of your company, your clientele, your office or building. Let your vision soar to the highest heights of your imagination, then live it!

---- ✪ ----

What Does Your Business Look Like?

---- ✪ ----

*When will you
or did you start?
Write in the date.*

_____

*Where is the
location?*

_____

*Do you have
employees? How
many?*

_____

*Who is your
market? Your
customers?*

_____

*What is your
market?*

_____

*What type of
marketing plan do
you have?*

_____

*How much money
does it cost to be
in business?*

_____

*How much money
does your com-
pany make a year?*

_____

*What is the one
thing your com-
pany does better
than any other*

_____

PART TWO: VISION

YELLOW BRICK ROAD
The Road To Success

---❈---

*"It is nothing to find no starting place in the world;
you just start from where you find yourself."*
      – August Wilson, playwright

*"The road to success is not paved with gold, glitter,
or greatness. You pave it that way."*
      – Robert S. Shumake

---❈---

57

Follow! Follow! Follow!
The Yellow Brick Road

To follow the Yellow Brick Road to success
you've got to have a lion's courage;
You've got to have more heart than a tin man
to stand the road test of success.

Develop your wit and clean
the straw from your mind;
Make sure there are no curtains,
for you to hide behind.

To win, you've got to stay on track.
Open your mouth shout loud and crow.
Don't be scared! Don't turn back!
Tell everybody and ask everywhere you go
for directions and corrections - don't depart.
The Yellow Brick Road can't be aimlessly
roamed.
So pack plenty of courage and take heart
If you stay on this road it will take you home.

SUCCESS!!!

One day as my children and I were watching "The Wizard of Oz," a powerful "Aha! Moment" blasted through my brain like a tornado.

My mouth literally gaped when I realized, this classic movie speaks directly to our experience as entrepreneurs. From start to finish, it blew my mind as I put the cast of characters, the plot and the concept into the context of life and business.

Won't you take this mind trip with me to my Emerald Epiphany.

At the beginning, we notice Dorothy. She's got a plan — to enjoy her idyllic life and protect her dog, Toto, from the mean lady who tries to take him away. Dorothy trusts the people around her to help: Auntie Em, her uncle and the folks around the farm in Kansas.

Think of your entrepreneurial self as Dorothy — you've got your business plan, trying to protect your assets and work with your team, when all of a sudden — Catastrophe strikes!

A tornado rips through your life, sucking you and your foundation up into dizzying oblivion. That's what happened to Dorothy.

Then you crash down in a place that's completely foreign. Or is it?

The great success guru Napoleon Hill

wrote in his book, Think and Grow Rich: "Every adversity, every failure and every heartache carries with it the Seed of an equivalent or greater Benefit."

That's Dorothy's story, and our own when everything seems to crash and burn. Because like the phoenix rising from the ashes, we are stronger and smarter and better prepared for success when we persevere through catastrophe.

And that's what Dorothy does, starting from the time she lands in Oz. That's where she finds the beginning of The Yellow Brick Road. It looks like the swirl at the center of a peppermint candy — starting out miniscule, then circling, circling, until it becomes an actual road.

"Wow!" I exclaimed as I watched this with my kids.

The swirling start of our entrepreneurial path begins with a brainstorm, a brilliant idea, that circles, circles, 'round and 'round in our brains, until it forms a real path of action to bring our dream into reality.

But, the key is we have to follow the plan. We have to continue amid the fear that wants to grip our mind. We must seek for wisdom to carry our business through, even when we ourselves do not feel smart enough, trained enough, or knowledgeable enough. We are on a path to success, which is meant to bring us to the yellow or might I say, the golden road.

GOALS

"The tragedy of life doesn't lie in not reaching your goal. The tragedy lies in having no goal to reach."

– Benjamin E. Mays, Educator

"A person with a goal will accomplish it regardless of physical, mental or emotional circumstances."

– Robert S. Shumake

A MAN WITH A GOAL is like a pack of hungry wolves that will not rest until they have found food.

A MAN WITH A GOAL is like a meteor on its way to the earth with enough power to create an earthquake.

A MAN WITH A GOAL is like a fist ready to smash his opponent's face – K.O.!

A MAN WITH A GOAL is like a prayer intended for a particular individual. Amen!

A MAN WITH A GOAL is like a basketball aimed toward a net – SWISH!

A MAN WITH A GOAL has the ability to impact the world because he has the power to stay on his path when others can't.

Amoment at the airport seemed ordinary, but in a flash such a powerful statement was made about human beings, it made me blink with revelation.

I was standing in a long line, waiting to check in for my flight. The ticket agent for Northwest Airlines was standing behind the counter steadily checking the passengers identification and their luggage.

"Have your ticket and I.D. out," the male agent barked, "and know your destination!" Those last four words echoed in my head because it just didn't make any sense to me. Why would he tell me to know where I'm going? How could I NOT know where I was going?!?

I mean, I had a specific purpose for this trip — to fly to Los Angeles, California, to meet with a major business person who woluld help me execute a specific real estate deal. Period. I knew what time I would arrive; How long I was going to stay; The hotel I'd chosen to accommodate me; What time we would arrive for our dinner reservations at The Ivy, and the specific time of my departing flight three days later.

But now, in the airport, my eyebrows drew together in confusion as the ticket agent repeated: "Know your destination!"

Then a lightbulb glowed in my head, shining a spotlight on the meaning of his message.

Oh, I thought, some people are getting on an airplane and they're not sure of their destination. But that still didn't vibe with me. It made no sense.

Sometimes we get in a car and have a vague idea where the restuarant or shoe store is located. We drive to the general area and ask someone for directions. Then we continue driving until we find it.

But an airplane?

The act of planning a trip and purchasing a ticket requires you to know exactly what airport and in what city you're flying to.

Doesn't it?

I was still perplexed when it was my turn to approach the ticket counter. So I asked the agent,

"Why do you tell people to know their destination?"

The man let out a pessimistic laugh. "I know it sounds ridiculous," he said, "But you wouldn't believe how many people in a day come up here and say, 'I know I'm going to Florida, but I don't know what city.'"

My eyes bugged. My head leaned slightly forward, like, say that again?

The man laughed. "I guess it's a sad commentary on life," he said, "flying aimlessly through the sky without a clue."

The man added that e-tickets only made it worse. Without a piece of paper that outlined their travel plan and reminded folks of where they were going, they seemed literally lost in space.

And so began my "Aha! moment" of the month.

As entrepreneurs, we cannot succeed without a business plan. In fact, statistics show that the average business fails within three years, usually because it lacks a focus or has lost the focus it began with. Without clearly defined goals and objectives — your destination — will cause you as a business person to fail to accomplish your purpose and mission.

This reminds me of what a wise man said when asked, "How important is it to have goals?"

His reply: "More important than a beating heart."

That's why I write out my goals in both my personal plan and my business plan. Actually, they're interchangeable. The title? "The Island Plan."

That's right! This brother wants to own an island. As you can see, I think far above and beyond most folks' capacity who see only Tattoo and Mr. Roark of television fame as worthy of calling a Fantasy Island their home.

But God blessed me with vision, to see the unseen, to believe that what I create in my imagination can be my reality.

As long as I make a plan, work the plan, pray and have faith, I believe that I, too, can own an island. My first step to making that happen is to write it down. Thus, "The Island Plan."

Why do I need an island?

Well, even though I love my work, I crave rest and relaxation in a place that's beautiful and recharges my battery, so that I may return to work at turbo-speed. And, I love to entertain friends and family in unique ways.

My island get-away will afford all of the above. My plan has clearly defined steps to actually buy and own my island.

For starters, I frequently communicate with real estate agents who specialize in selling islands. I have identified exactly how much profit my business needs to generate in order to purchase "Refresher Island." My island will have all the toys and luxuries that define my personal slice of paradise. I've named the boat I'll buy, I know which jet skis I'll purchase, I've even consulted with an architect to design and build my house exactly to my desires.

It's not a secret that I keep this plan close to me at all times. My friends and family know about it; they share the dream now and they will be the ones basking in the sun and splashing in the surf when it becomes reality.

My point?

If your business is not growing and prospering the way you desire, perhaps the problem is that you have not developed your Island Plan. Remember that your Island Plan should be bigger than what you have or see right now. Make it a goal that you can experience only through putting the plan into action.

Because the difference between doing business, and having a "bidness," is the plan. The difference between success and failure is the plan. Your plan may need to be stretched. You can revise it. When it appears that it is not working. Rethink. Rewrite. Start again and succeed.

So whether you're just thinking about your new business, or struggling after three years to make it prosper, or looking for ways to improve...

Remember what the ticket agent said: "Know your destination."

Do that by writing out a concise business plan that details short-term and long-term goals.

And when you plan your work, and work your plan, it's only a matter of time before you're waking up on your own Fantasy Island.

Developing Goals

*Immediate
Personal Goals
(within the year)*

_____

_____

_____

_____

_____

_____

_____

_____

*Immediate
Business Goals
(within 2 years)*

_____

_____

_____

_____

_____

_____

_____

Dreams

"When your dreams turn to dust, vacuum."
— Bishop Desmond Tutu

"Dreams are God's way of allowing man to come as close to the tree of life as possible."
— Robert S. Shumake

Dance and sing, do your thing!

Reach for stars, savor life,
    sweet as candy bars.

Express passion, imagine the
    size of the prize to mes-
    merize your eyes.

Accept yourself, your wealth.

Make magic, you have it!

A serial killer is on the loose, and he's coming after you. His name is Fred E.A. Ripper, a.k.a. F.E.A.R.

And the reason he wants to get you is, he's in charge of the wealthiest place in the world. If you had to guess where that is, you might say, Fort Knox or the Fiji Islands or the Rothchild Family Trust or Bill Gates' bank accounts.

Wrong!

The wealthiest place in the world is THE GRAVEYARD! That's where millions of poor souls are buried with billion-dollar dreams unfilled.

And that's why Fred E.A. Ripper wants to take you there. He wants to steal the money tree that's rooted in your dreams.

See, Mr. Ripper is a pretty smart dude. You talk about a con artist! He has a way of slinking into your life, sneaking up on you when you least expect it, and bam! He's gotcha with moments of doubt, anxiety attacks, and straight-up quitting thoughts.

But I know a secret about Mr. Ripper. He's a fraud. He's one of those cats who knows how to make you believe the hype. He can seduce like the slickest Casanova; some folks actually get addicted to his fear vibe. They're so used to being under his spell, they can't shake it. Even though they know he is out to rob them and kill their dream, they remain under his spell.

Then Fred E.A. Ripper wins! He runs off to the graveyard with your treasure and buries it forever. At night, he retreats to his tomb and greedily gloats over his huge stock of great ideas, exceptional products and multimillion dollar enterprises.

Let's think about it: what's our relationship with Fred E.A. Ripper, Fear? We all know him. He visits me daily. Though I've learned to live with him, I REFUSE to let him win. He might slow me down at times, but I always beat him down with optimism and a positive attitude. That's my Kryptonite against this Superman's Evil Twin.

Because when I defeat him, I am Superman in my personal and professional life.

Here's an example.

Wait, first let me explain, Fred (Fear) is a pretty schizophrenic dude. He's got some other personalities that always show up at the worst time. One side of his sick personality is known as Fear of Success. Fear of Success plagues me and every entrepreneur on the planet.

This aspect of Mr. F.E.A.R. paid me a visit the day I was supposed to close on a beautiful new home on a lake. I had the closing check in my pocket as I drove to the 6500-square-foot-house that I wanted to call home. It was the perfect deal, and I was excited to reach this milestone in my life.

But suddenly, Fred infiltrated my thoughts.

He hissed twisted things such as, "You were homeless as a kid. You squatted in unheated houses, just to have a roof over your head. Why do you think you deserve a big, pretty house on a lake?"

For too long, I let Mr. Fear of Success seduce me into thinking maybe I shouldn't buy the house. I drove around the lake a couple times. All the while, the seller was blowing up my phone, trying to reach me to seal the deal. Yet, I didn't call him back for two days, simple put, I was caught in the clutches of Mr. Fear of Success.

But the real Robert Shumake finally stared him down. And Fred E.A. Ripper, aka. Fear disappeared.

Well, almost.

See, in every situation where Mr. Fear appears, I realize, I can't kill him completely. Like an evil, haunting spirit, it's nearly impossible to exorcise him from the human mind and soul. So I have a trick that's as good as a stake through his heart.

I envision myself stuffing Mr. FEAR into a large suitcase. It's invisible, and within my imagination, I can carry it anywhere -- into a board room or a restaurant, onto an airplane, and up to a podium when I speak before thousands of people.

My point? Mr. Ripper is always with me. I carry FEAR around like baggage. And we all do. But I keep him in his place — sealed up and trapped where he can't do me any harm.

Fear of Success is a particularly wicked concept for us entrepreneurs. Why are we making the effort to produce excellent products and services, craft a brand that's memorable and respected, and earn the financial security and freedom that everyone craves? Why do it if we're ultimately terrified of the very thing we're seeking?

It's a horrific contradiction in what we do. But it's there, so we have to deal with it. The trick is to know that. Recognize when Mr. FEAR of Success pays a visit. Did you suddenly fall ill just before that important presentation? Did you deliberately miss a deadline, knowing it would sour your great relationship with an important client?

Go easy on yourself. The important thing is to figure out why you feel this way. With soul-searching and self-analysis, you'll discover how fear enters in. Then you'll know how to keep Mr. FEAR of Success in his place.

And even during those moments when Fred E.A. Ripper stings you with paralyzing force, take a deep breath, focus your mind on the vision, and say out loud: "I gotta do it! Now!"

At the same time, call your dream team; their words of encouragement will pull you from the shadows of doubt and make you shout to the world that you're ready to impress with success. Pray, and write out your feelings.

All this will keep you safe from the wicked ways of Fred E.A. Ripper. And your dreams will shine in the light, creating prosperity for you and a better way for the world.

On the next page, you'll find an exercise that will help you hold tight to your ambitions and desires — and enjoy the riches of your dreams!

*List all the things
you've dreamed of
doing. Making a
list will stabilize your
dreams so they can-
not escape you.*

_____

_____

_____

_____

*Review your list.
Rearrange your
dreams, in numerical
order, with your most
passionate dream
as #1.*

_____

_____

_____

_____

_____

*Through your circle
of influence, identify
individuals who can
help you obtain your
dreams. List people
you know, and people
in the industry whom
you will pursue.*

_____

_____

_____

_____

_____

*Create a schedule
for achieving your
dreams.*

_____

_____

You Can Do It!

_____

_____

_____

_____

E AGLES

"You can't soar like an eagle if you hang around chickens."

— *African Proverb*

"If you walk around pecking at the ground, you'll never see the fruit in the trees."

— *Robert S. Shumake*

EAGLES have strong wings, sharp claws,
and KEEN VISION.

EAGLES are regal and unique.

EAGLES have ATTITUDE, and

EAGLES take ACTION!

EAGLES fly close to GOD.
They soar high and AIM HIGH.

EAGLES are family birds, and helping birds.

EAGLES SUPPORT.

EAGLES are flying experts. They either FLY
or die! There is no in-between.

EAGLES SUCCEED by doing what other
eagles DO!

EAGLES that don't are merely chickens.

H ave you ever seen a fat eagle?
What about a fat turkey, chicken or
pigeon?

A recent outing to the zoo with my children got me thinking about these birds, and how each one reflects human nature.

It's pretty wild to think about.

First, I looked into the eyes of an American Eagle. Talk about focus! That bird stared at me with such intensity, I felt it was reading my mind. And it sat so proudly — straight and tall, yellow beak high, its talons firmly gripping the solid log at the center of its exhibit. It seemed to move in unison with its partner, observing us humans as if we were on exhibit for them! With each turn of its head, the Eagle displayed a majestic spread of feathers framing its proud face. Its body? Lean and streamlined.

I walked away, awed by the aura of confidence that the bird had projected toward me. That bird knew it had an important purpose, and wasn't about to get off course.

After that, my family and I headed to the Farmyard. On the way, flocks of pigeons waddled across our path, pecking at the dirt to chomp down bits of popcorn, discarded hot dog buns and a melting ice cream sandwich. Some of the pigeons were so fat from devouring garbage all day long, they looked like feathered balls on tiny stick legs.

A short time later, we watched chickens and turkeys peck at the ground, constantly eating seeds off the dusty dirt. Their feet and some of their feathers were soiled. Their heads stayed down. And they ate constantly. As a result, some were quite plump. They had no consciousness that their sole purpose on the planet, in human's eyes, was to fatten up for slaughtering, seasoning and serving to the masses to devour. At the moment, they seemed quite happy to eat all day long and not think about their fate.

In my mind an, "Aha! Moment" flashed like an imaginary neon sign. I couldn't help but compare each of these birds to people.

Which one are you? An eagle, a pigeon, a chicken or a turkey?

Entrepreneurs should all strive to be like an eagle, the crown prince of the bird family; the symbol of American liberty and power. But too many of us function like pigeons, chickens and turkeys.

And it's all about lifestyle.

As an entrepreneur, it's time to take a hard look at your lifestyle. Are you fattening up, and unwittingly preparing yourself for the slaughter of failure or bankruptcy? Or are you focused and regal like the eagle?

How often do we go through life fattened by what the world gives us? Fattened with ignorance through false information. Fattened by hours of destructive television watching. Fattened by negative madness.

Consider for a moment the mental, physical nonproductive fattening habits you have acquired. Remember that turkeys and chickens are fattened for the specific purpose of being devoured. Recognize how your mental and emotional views are priming you for the slaughter. Know that what fattens you up, weighs you down.

Now, visualize the eagle. There is not one ounce of fat. He's a lean, mean, flying machine. You can't get close enough to eagles to entice them to eat the dirty grain prepared for chickens. Eagles soar high, collecting the wholesome meal befitting its power. The eagle demands respect. If you want to fly high like an eagle, you've got to lose weight mentally, spiritually, and physically. Drop the weight of negative thinking. Trim the fat of accepting average accomplishments. Commit yourself to a lean productive life-style. Put these ideas into action as an entrepreneur.

Evaluate your business for areas you need to trim, then perform liposuction on the business flab. Is the company weighed down by too much overhead? Are you indulging in extravagant expenses for entertainment, office maintenance, or taxes?

Pin point solutions. For example, if you need to gather better information from your accountant to guide your business more efficiently, then do so.

Be an eagle! Trim the fat... and FLY HIGH!

❖

Make a list of things to trim from your personal and business expenses.

❖

_____

_____

_____

_____

_____

_____

_____

_____

_____

_____

_____

_____

_____

_____

_____

_____

_____

SURVIVAL SKILLS

FOR

VISIONARY

ENTREPRENEURS

SURVIVAL SKILLS FOR
VISIONARY ENTREPRENEURS

Keep visualizing your dreams and believe that you can achieve them. Cultivating a positive outlook is not as easy as you think, since many people are worriers. Practice being positive every day.

Surround yourself with affirming people – family, business associates and employees.

Defend yourself against negative people who say, "I told you so." This may require ingenuity if you are married to or living with a pessimist.

Celebrate every sign of progress. Congratulate yourself each time the business improves, even if you miss your goal.

Make quality your top priority. Accept only excellence from your employees and your product.

Know everything about your product.

Nurture relationships with your customer base. Develop coupons, special discounts and celebration days to keep and show appreciation for their business.

Follow your business plan closely, unless you're changing

it to perfect your business. Organize your activities so that you are following your business plan. Be engrossed in every aspect of your business. No area is too trivial or too complex to learn.

Understand and comply with laws and regulations governing your business.

It's okay to take the road less traveled, provided you have researched it thoroughly and mapped a strategic route.

Have a clearly identified target market. Know your competition, their proximity to you, their product's features, benefits and prices. Study their successful marketing and advertising methods.

Keep abreast of new trends and changes in your field.

PART THREE

FAITH

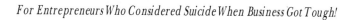

Now Faith is the substance of things hoped for,
and the evidence of things not seen.
– Hebrews 11th part , verse 1 (KJV)

PART THREE: FAITH

If you watched a movie called The Robert Shumake Story, my rags-to-riches rise would make your jaw drop. That's how I feel when I reflect on the past 15 years.

Imagine, being so poor that we didn't have heat! Sleeping in our clothes! Hearing the icy crackle of porcelain when my brother's hot urine caused the frozen toilet bowl to split! Then, at one point, being homeless and desperate — we "squatted" in an abandoned, unheated house!

Now flash forward. Not only do I own a 6,500-square foot house on a private lake, but I'm building a vacation home in the Dominican Republic. Every day I go to work in a beautiful office building that I designed and constructed for my company! On top of that, I'm the landlord for several other businesses that rent space in my building. Not to mention, I deal in real estate and development from coast to coast.

So I took what some may view as a tragic aspect of my childhood, and I tranformed it into triumph as an adult and businessman.

But how?

Let the phenomenal past president of Morehouse College, Benjamin Elijah Mays, answer that. He taught that we should measure a person's strength by how well he overcomes obstacles.

Clearly I have strength. But where does it come from?

Faith.

Plain and simple.

Because to me, our unheated house was a palace. My mother was a queen and my father was a king. In our royal, loyal and loving family I was taught to think of myself as a prince. And even though we had no furnace, and went without MichCon heat for years, we survived. Love, plus kerosene heaters, kept our rooms toasty.

Still, going into unheated rooms meant facing the Michigan winter hawk. It was ruthless. Sometimes we were so cold, we slept in our clothes. And the only way to warm the toilet seat was to scoot back and forth on it before plunking down our bare bottoms. That's how my younger brother cracked the toilet bowl.

It's comical now.

And, while our childhood might sound horrific to some, my brothers, my sister and I view it as a blessing. Because what we lacked in heat we made up for with faith and love.

My mother, who I believe has as much faith as Jesus Christ, instilled strong faith in us kids. In fact, all of my siblings are ministers.

And me, well, I am profoundly appreciative of how the challenges of my childhood prepared me for awesome achievements in adulthood.

I would not edit or remake a single scene in The Robert Shumake Story.

Those obstacles gave me strength and

developed character and fortitude in me. They still encourage me to seek the best and be the best.

Back when we were shivering in our house, we had faith that one day we would enjoy round-the-clock heat. We had faith that we would own a home. As a child with asthma, I had faith that one day it would be controlled and I would feel better. Today, I have faith that my real estate and development business, and my scholarship fund, will continue to attract stellar success.

But what, exactly, is faith?

"Unquestioning belief that does not require proof or evidence," according to Webster's dictionary.

But I'll tell you this: once you have faith, and you see its power coming to fruition in your life in dollars, business deals and miraculous circumstances, you'll no longer question the definition of faith.

You'll simply know.

So the next time you look at a situation in your life and think it's terrible, have faith that it's happening for an important reason. It's preparing you, strengthening you for the next great accomplishment. It's honing your character, giving you valuable insight so that you may be a better person and smarter entrepreneur.

Faith is our fuel, our tool, our rock.

It's the key word in the script for The Robert Shumake Story.

So think about the movie of your life. If you want to live happily make faith the guiding force in all that you do. It will cause you to experience great forevers.

List Obstacles Blocking Your Success

_____

_____

_____

_____

_____

_____

_____

_____

_____

Brainstorm Powerful Solutions

_____

_____

_____

_____

_____

_____

_____

_____

F EAR

"Our greatest fears are often of the things that do not happen."
— Benjamin E. Mays, Educator

"Fear and faith have a lot in common; they both say that what you cannot see will happen to you."
— Stacy Foster, Senior Pastor
Life Changers International Ministries,
Detroit, Michigan

"Fear will trespass on worthwhile imagination."
— Robert S. Shumake

FEAR is...

Failure to step out in faith.

Exchanging your greatness for the void of mediocrity.

A stumble in darkness.

Running from victory, from faith, from the brilliant sparkle of success.

───────────── ─────────────

Fear is nothing more than the silhouette of ourselves outside of the brilliance of the sun.

───────────── ─────────────

Batman taught me something about fear. You have to face it and embrace it. That's the only way to get over it. It was certainly mind-blowing having this deep revelation as I sat in the dark movie theater watching "Batman Begins."

But Bruce Wayne had a lesson for all of us, especially entrepreneurs.

As a kid, remember, he fell into that hole near Wayne Manor, where a flock of black bats attacked him. From then on, terror haunted him at every turn. Bedtime, for him was horrific. The fear was so compelling that he asked his parents to leave the theatre early. They did, and in the alley, a mugger fatally shot his mom and dad. Of course, Bruce blamed his paralyzing fear for helping to steal the lives of his parents.

As an adult, he searches the world for answers. Finally, a martial arts master tells him he has to embrace his fears.

We then see Bruce standing tall as dozens of bats fly right at him. He stands taller, undaunted by that he had once feared.

Facing his biggest fear cures him. As a result, he finds the power within to fulfill his destiny, becoming Batman; Conquering his fear, then, empowers him to be used to save the world.

My "Aha! Moment" lightbulb glowed brilliantly as I watched this.

Because, like an ominous flock of bats, fear is a giant that follows you everywhere you go. It's like an invisible creature overshadowing your every step, your every move. Fear is a bully. In the dark areas of your mind, fear waits, ready to steal God's gifts from you.

Fear is tricky; it knows when you're most vulnerable — during your in-between times. You see, fear can only come out when shade blocks the sun.

When we question the power of God's rays of sunshine, all those question marks allow fear to slip in through the cracks in our faith.

Fear can move like that, because it's nothing more than the silhouette of ourselves when we step away from the brilliance of the sun. Fear magnifies the moment we walk closer to darkness. It casts shadows over our thoughts and possibilities, telling us what we can't do. Fear breeds negative visions that convince us that our ideas will fail. Fear speaks bad dialogue inside our brains: "People won't buy my product. No one will like it. I might as well give up."

Any idea is valid when someone believes in it. I mean, look at the Pet Rock as an example. Someone came up with what might sound ridiculous. But millions of people enthusiastically purchased Pet Rocks, and proudly displayed them in homes and offices. Go figure!

The inventor had faith in the idea, and fearlessly proceeded to produce and sell it — with phenomenal success.

My pastor loves to remind us: fear and faith have the same power — they force us to believe in things we cannot see. They are opposite extremes, constantly jocking for domination in our minds. One is light, one is night. One is the sun, one is the dark side of the moon.

PART THREE: FAITH

But fear's shadow is not faith's reality.
Let faith dominate.
STAY IN THE SUNLIGHT!!!

WHAT SHADOWS YOUR SUCCESS?

Need for a Mentor? Write the names and contact information of three people who are doing what you are doing or want to do.

_____

_____

_____

Call them, arrange an appointment and speak with them about your project.

Need for more knowledge? Attend a conference or seminar (check local papers)

_____

Hire people with the knowledge you seek — i.e. an accountant, a marketing company, etc.

_____

Need to make a change? List ways to improve.

_____

_____

_____

Commit to dates and actions to make these changes.

Action I _____ Date_____

Action 2 _____ Date_____

PART THREE: FAITH

PLANTING SEEDS

"You can't be a tree by hanging out with the bushes."

> – James C. Perkins, pastor
> Greater Christ Baptist Church - Detroit, MI

"The seeds that you plant will determine the amount of ripe fruit that you pick from the tree."

> – Robert S. Shumake

YOU REAP WHAT YOU SOW are powerful words. Why? Because if you are planting eagle seeds in your mind, then your vision will be "Sky."

If you **plant seeds** in your heart with the fight of a stallion, then the world will stand aside as you claim your gold medallion.

If you **plant seeds** that say, "I Can," you will be planting miracles with your own tiny hands.

If you **plant seeds** of disenchantment, fear and despair, the universe will never know your dreams, and assume they aren't there.

If you **plant seeds** of courage, laughter and success, a mighty tree will grow. Neither a pine nor a sap, but a tree called, **"Blessed."**

Every entrepreneur endures moments when all your hard work seems fruitless. Despite weeks, months and years of cultivating your business, it seems the money and bigger clients and recognition will never come. When I first started my business, I had too many of those times to count. But this story always renewed my faith that one day, my business would grow and become a multimillion dollar global empire.

The story is about a wise farmer who told his two apprentices:

"Take these seeds, plant them on your own farms, and water them every day."

Both apprentices followed his instructions. For a full year, they watered the ground where they had planted the seeds.

But nothing grew.

Apprentice #1 got discouraged and said, "Forget it. These seeds are bad." He stopped watering them. In fact, he gave up farming altogether.

But Apprentice #2 had faith. After a year of watering — with no plant in sight — he summoned an expert to teach him more about these particular seeds. The expert studied the soil. After careful observation, he prescribed the following: "Water, please."

Apprentice #2 followed those directions. One

day, while walking to the well to get water, he passed Apprentice #1.

"Why are you going to well," Apprentice #1 asked, "since the seeds that Farmer Joe gave us were bad?"

A smile was all the response Apprentice #2 gave. He continued to the well, and kept watering his seeds.

Still, no sign of a single sprout had appeared.

And, that had the town laughing hysterically at Apprentice #2 who watered the soil daily with no results. Some folks even said he should be committed to an insane asylum.

But still he watered the soil.

Five years passed, then 10, then 20, but nothing grew.

Finally the ground broke, and a little gold leaf appeared. Seven days later, there stood a 40 foot money tree.

The towns people watched in amazement. "How in the world did you grow this money tree?" they asked.

"Well, you must be faithful and follow instructions," the Apprentice answered. "Whatever you plant, be consistent, persevere, and water the seeds. Perhaps, you'll find that a money tree grows in money mud."

So, then Apprentice #2 had the last laugh. Yep, he laughed himself all the way to the bank.

SOMETIMES

"Your failures in life come from not realizing your nearness to success when you gave up."
– Yoruba Proverb

"As long as there is WILL left in the spirit, one can go on."
– Robert S. Shumake

SOMETIMES I FEEL like the whole world is against me.

My boss doesn't appreciate my work.

My spouse just wants to complain.

My kids are constantly asking for things.

My friends are telling me their problems.

My Church is preaching to somebody else.

My family expects for me to handle everything all by myself.

The world seems so against me. But as long as I'm not against myself...

I WILL SUCCEED.

Write a Positive Letter To Yourself

_____

_____

_____

_____

_____

_____

_____

_____

_____

_____

_____

_____

_____

_____

_____

_____

_____

_____

_____

_____

Y OUR TINY HANDS

"Everyone is more or less the master of his own fate."

– Aesop, Griot

"We must realize that our inevitable outcome is held in our own tiny hands."

– Robert S. Shumake

Only your tiny hands
     Others may not believe,
     But, if you don't
     it will never be.

     Your friends can push you,
     But, if you don't move,
     It is wasted time indeed.

     Leaders can show you the way,
     And yet, the choice is yours.
     You must follow the plan.

     It doesn't matter who does what for you,
     Who believes in you, or fights for you,
     Your destination, your success, or your
     failure awaits in your own tiny hands.

L ook at your hands. Turn them so that you're cupping them upward, side by side, as if you're holding a double palmful of gold coins.

Because the power of your tiny hands is worth far more than that. It's immeasurable. Cradled in your tiny hands lies the power to change the world.

My siblings and I proved that as kids, when we held the monthly Shumake Olympics in our neighborhood. Now I'm proving it once again, by hosting the Robert S. Shumake Scholarship Relays to raise a million dollars in scholarships for future entrepreneurs across the world. Visit our website, www.shumakerelays.com to learn more about this premier track and field meet.

It all began with the four tiny sets of hands attached to the Shumake children. See, in our inner-city neighborhood, we didn't have much to do.

Though we had toys, our parents encouraged us to use our imaginations to create activities to ward off boredom.

Boy, did we have a ball! Who knew making our own toys and developing our own games would show us the time of our lives?

For example, we made a merry-go-round by getting in the clothes dryer and spinning around and around.

Once a month, we held "The Shumake Olympics."

Talk about innovation! For the softball throw, we used a softball that my younger brother found at the playground. For the standing broad jump, my sister used a wooden yardstick and a pencil to measure precise leaps.
Hurdles? We placed a broomstick over milk crates.

"The Shumake Olympics" — engineered and hosted by four little kids — eventually attracted participants from across town.

We even created ribbons and medals as awards for contestants.

Now, as an adult, it's humbling to come across folks who participated in our Olympics. They still grin with fond memories of all the fun. And many perfected their skills because four little kids used their big hearts, creative minds, and tiny hands to create priceless childhood memories.

Today, I'm executing that concept on a global scale.

I'm planning The Second Annual Robert S. Shumake Scholarship Relays — a sanctioned track meet that will raise $100,000 for scholarships. The success of the first annual event blew my mind!

On that sunny April morning, I stood in awe as 450 athletes from 25 schools converged on the track and field at Martin Luther King, Jr. High School in Detroit.

It's the largest private high school track and field meet in Michigan. And I'm aiming to make it the largest private track meet in the Midwest.

I have faith that The Robert S. Shumake Scholarship Relays will get bigger and better every year. And I WILL reach the million-dollar mark so that I may give much needed scholarships to future entrepreneurs around the world. It's all in my tiny hands.

Just as your greatest successes — or failures — await their fate in your two palms. You can have an imagination that rivals Steven Spielberg, but without action with your hands, it's a worthless and tragic waste of talent.

God took action and created the world in six days.

I'm putting my global vision to work.

What are you doing to improve your world by using what's at the end of your arms? Yes, God gave us hands to mold, to shape, to build, and to execute our ideas. It may take us longer than six days to create our own new world, but we can build or destroy our destiny with just our tiny hands. You've got what it takes. Make it happen!

---❈---

List Several Actions You Will Take To Secure Your Customer Base

---❈---

_____

_____

_____

_____

_____

_____

_____

_____

_____

_____

_____

_____

_____

_____

_____

SURVIVAL SKILLS

FOR

FAITHFUL
ENTREPRENEURS

Be highly motivated and confident of your ability to succeed in business.

People skills will take you a long way. Develop them!

Have faith that you can and will overcome any setbacks that come your way.

Remember, others have had to overcome, too.

Change the word "problem" to "challenge" each time you face difficulty. Challenges are what life is about.

Seek counsel from supportive, trusting friends and acquaintances.

Stay upbeat. Don't walk around looking worried; that might make those who work with you nervous and unsure about their jobs.

Review your business plan. Modify it as needed to reverse setbacks, and to improve forecasting.

Take a drive, see a movie, take a nap, etc. to unwind and clear your mind. You will come back to the challenge with clearer insight.

PART FOUR

Perseverance

STRENGTH TO WIN

"You have to know you can win. You have to think you can win. You have to feel you can win."
— *Sugar Ray Leonard, Boxer*

"One step takes you from wishing to doing."
— *Robert S. Shumake*

THE STRENGTH TO WIN IS...

To never think lose.
To never see failure.

THE STRENGTH TO WIN...

Begins the moment you start
Knowing that once begun
You won't depart,
Until you've given your all.

THE STRENGTH TO WIN IS...

A force inside, compelling,
Motivating and confirming
An attitude of Victory.

THE STRENGTH TO WIN IS...

To see beyond the present,
Amid all uncertainty,
Visualizing your unconquerable end.

Purpose plus mission,
Fueled by vision,
With faith in yourself,
and a plan to contend,
Persevering to the end,
That is...

THE STRENGTH TO WIN!

H ave you ever met someone from the *"I'm Gonna Tribe"*?

It's a worldwide family of people who share a single distinguishing characteristic.

The skin color can be any hue of the amazing human spectrum around the globe. They represent vastly diverse cultures and religions.

In fact, this Tribe has millions of descendants; many of those men and women live in your community.

People in the I'm Gonna Tribe dream about entrepreneurship, but membership in their Tribe typically prohibits courageous business ventures.

You'll know why when you learn the only way to recognize someone in the I'm Gonna Tribe.

It's in the way they talk.

They typically tell you, "Some day I'm going to learn money management and open my own financial planning service." Or you might hear another member say, "Someday I'm gonna apply for a grant to open a children's museum." Others say things like, "I'm gonna go back to school" and "I'm gonna buy a better house" and "I'm gonna get myself together."

"I'm gonna quit this job I hate." "I'm gonna write my business plan." "I'm gonna secure the funds to open a chain of fitness centers." The problem is they never do.

Instead, their biggest accomplishments remain in their imaginations. Because folks in the I'm Gonna Tribe can come up with some really fantastic, creative concepts.

I know one brother who told me about a barber shop that would offer a personal shopping service, and serve while-you-wait meals in the adjoining restaurant.

But when I saw him five years later, this dude was still working his ordinary job, still talking about the dream business he was GONNA open.

You'll notice, members of the I'm Gonna Tribe are also really good at talking stuff. Yet, they often lack the *"Action Gene"* that us real entrepreneurs are blessed with. Because if it weren't for the Action Gene, we'd all still be unhappy, unproductive members of the I'm Gonna Tribe. The I'm Gonna Tribe suffers from not taking action; that immobility causes a void in the world – *a nothingness.*

Just as they lack the Action Gene, they are also pumped with the deadly virus: FEAR.

Fear poisons the blood of the entrepreneurial spirit. When digested, it paralyzes its victims. It takes the tribal members hostage, holding them in I'm Gonna Hospice. There they sit, crippled by fear.

Have you ever been a member of the I'm Gonna Tribe? Have you ever considered joining the I'm Gonna Tribe? Their membership drives run 24-7. Be careful, don't let the virus catch you. Don't be convinced to join their pathetic bandwagon. I'd rather invite you to join my tribe.

It's a tribe at war with the I'm Gonnas. Sometimes they hate on us because they envy our Action Genes. They're also jealous when they notice how we get daily immunizations against the Fear virus. Sometimes, though, we inspire them to defect and join us victors.

My tribe?

NEVER SAY DIE!

This small, select group believes we have the strength to win, no matter what. We strive to overcome even the most bleak circumstances. We keep moving, conquering new lands, recruiting new minds, and building our strength.

We're on a mission – in hot pursuit. Our personal missions in business make us a mighty breed. Check us out. We are leading the world. We have passion and vision.

By reading this book, you are acknowledging your allegiance with the "Never Say Die" tribe. Stay focused. You are making a choice to belong to the best and the brightest. Claim your spot in the sun! Create your legacy of wealth and power. Make a positive mark on the world.

Do it now!

And Never Say Die.

POWER OF MY MIND

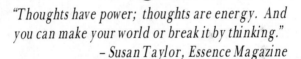

"Thoughts have power; thoughts are energy. And you can make your world or break it by thinking."
                              – Susan Taylor, Essence Magazine

"I never knew that I could create or destroy so much with just my little ole' mind."

                              – Robert S. Shumake

WITHIN MY MIND lies the power to win. I have the power to excel. My mind has the power of a champion, a victor, a leader, a fighter.

THE POWER OF MY MIND allows me to choose my destination. Success or failure. I chose success. A successful mind is my mind.

My mind is packed with knowledge of things discovered, invented, and accomplished by people; things that others thought were impossible for them to achieve.

THE POWER OF MY MIND defines my past, my present, and my future.

My mind always informs me that, if I am to accomplish anything, it will be through **THE POWER OF MY MIND.**

" Robert, how'd you start your business?" people ask me all the time.

"With a cell phone and an ink pen," I answer, realizing just how comical it was to launch my first company with no money and no written business plan.

But I had the confidence of Jean Claude Van Damme; I felt invincible. And my success today proves that.

But what I don't mention in these brief exchanges, however, is a crucial ingrendient.

Concentration.

Ask any entrepreneur, and they'll tell you that concentration -- actually OBSESSION -- fueled their initial quest to go into business.

By concentration and obsession I mean constantly thinking about what you'll do, how you'll do it, when you'll do it, and how you'll feel doing it.

Call it a leap of faith or blind pursuit of the American Dream.

Call it what you want.

I call it success.

And it all started from the power within. I'm not related to the Can't Brothers. I'm part of the Internal Fortitude Family.

Join me.

Let's obsess together on how to grow our businesses bigger and better by helping each other, and ultimately the world.

Perhaps, like me, all you'll need is a cell phone, an ink pen. But for sure you'll need lots of CONCENTRATION.

P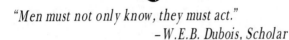ARALYZED

"Men must not only know, they must act."
– W.E.B. Dubois, Scholar

*"The only thing that keeps a person from ac-
complishing something is their inability to take
action."*

– Robert S. Shumake

PARALYSIS IS...

To know what needs to be
done and never to do –
afraid to try without a clue.

To be able to dream and
Yet, never live one out
To be a sleepwalker,
Roaming aimlessly about.

To see your goal
With your own eyes.
And make promises to yourself
That someday you'll try.

Feeling that burning desire to seek
After your very destiny,
But, too afraid to try,
Worried that success might not be.

E PIDEMIC STRIKES ENTREPRE-
NEURS! Get Vaccinated Now!
The Centers for Success Control report
that a virulent new strain of Procrastination
Flu is claiming millions of Entrepreneurs. This
year's bug is particularly horrific because it
causes what experts are calling "paralysis of
analysis." That's right, it will downright stop a
business person in his or her tracks. Yes, this bug
will knock them on their backs, and force them
into a comatose state. Promising new businesses
around the globe are falling into bankruptcy,
closing up shop and depriving the masses of
brilliant products and services.

"We've not seen such widespread in-
fection since the Failure Fever outbreak back
during the Depression," says Dr. B. Optimistic at
the Centers for Success Control. "We're urging
everyone to get vaccinnated immediately."

Doctors say you're especially at risk
for Procrastination Flu if you constantly entertain a "what if" mindset. That is, allowing your
thoughts to fester in feverish fits of doubt, worry
and doom will literally leave you weak in a don
nothing stupor. Another strain of the virus is
found among folks who repeatedly utter empty
phrases like, "One day I'm going to open my

beauty shop," or "When I get myself together, I'm going back to school to study business."

Experts also warn that the Procrastination Flu is extremely contagious. A sure-fire way to get infected with this destructive affliction is to hang around people who complain, criticize and waste time.

It's such an aggressive strain, life coaches continuously warn that it's striking down many entrepreneurs who -- by all accounts -- seemed well on their way to fame and fortune.

"Everyone is at risk," says Dr. Optimistic. "This year's Procrastination Flu bug is especially ruthless because it blindsides folks who thought they were making all the right moves."

Early symptoms of Procrastination Flu include: anxiety, worry, fear, confusion, isolation, depression and a sense of hopelessness. Then the ailment progresses to insomnia, temper flare-ups and an overwhelming sense of slipping into darkness.

Finally, the disease causes obsessive analysis of every detail of one's life and business. This obsessive behavior results in paralysis, as the entrepreneur becomes frozen with fear and doubt; he or she loses the strength to work, create, speak or in many cases, even pray.

"This is a dire emergency," Dr. Op-

timistic warns. "I am urging everyone, even those who, currently are cultivating a daily success mindset, to get vaccinated now. Don't risk dooming your brilliance to the graveyard."

The doctor says the vaccination involves a heavy dose of Faith, daily treatments of Positive Attitude, and hourly recitations of the mantra, "Do it now!"

At the same time, experts say you must make a thorough assessment of your professional health, so they can prescribe the best remedy for what ails you. Oftentimes, a thorough evaluation of the "What if?" levels in your brain will indicate exactly how you can boost your immunity against Procrastination Flu.

For example, if tests show a mass teeming with the words, "What if I had gone back to get that degree?" then your remedy is simply to enroll in school, now.

If you're suffering from an itchy rash from the words "What if I had created a business plan?" creeping over your thoughts, then consult with a successful entrepreneur to help you craft a powerful plan.

If your "what ifs" are cramping your gut because you didn't set aside money, then open a savings account now and begin setting aside a little each week. If you're constantly coughing, "What if I had marketed my business differently?" then your treatment is to hire an excellent marketing person.

As you take action to immunize your-self against Procrastination Flu, Dr. Optimistic says it's imperative that you also train your vocal cords to repeat, "Do it now!" throughout the day.

That will, he says, trigger your subconscious mind to erase all inklings toward putting things on the back burner. That only causes them to boil over and burn.

"Burns are another symptom of Procrastination Flu," he says, "because these entrepreneurs find themselves putting out fires that erupt when they don't take care of business right away."

The Center for Success Control stresses that every entrepreneur who succumbs to Procrastination Flu is inflicting loss and damage on a global scale.

"If you allow this bug to paralyze your talent, the world will never benefit from your brilliance," says Dr. Optimistic. "Treat yourself with the above-mentioned immunity-boosters, and wash them down with loud repetitions of 'Do it now!'"

Don't let Procrastination Flu get you!

Make a
commitment
to yourself that
your life
is going to
change.

_____

_____

_____

_____

_____

_____

Focus on
what needs to
happen for
the change.

_____

_____

_____

_____

Develop
possible
reasons to help
you overcome
any obstacles
concerning
your vision.

_____

_____

_____

_____

_____

_____

I can

"I can."
   – Charles Wesley, Historian

"Once a person realizes his full potential, he can't be confined to the world's limitations."
   – Robert S. Shumake

I CAN be whatever I set my mind to be.

I CAN have all of the things that I commit
myself to have.

I CAN become a winner, simply by
believing that a Winner
lives and loves in me.

Y ou can speak your way to success.
How? By learning the language of achievement.

I speak it, and my family speaks it.

Athletes follow the same creed. They know it's the key to the secret language of success, too. Those four letters hold all the power in the world when it comes to being excellent and winning. You see, when you speak the language of success to yourself and others, you can beat the biggest, brawniest opponent in the game of life. That goes for linebackers, golfers, CEOs and lawyers alike.

So what's Word #1 in the Language of Success?

I CAN!

Now, what's the vicious syllable that's banned from the vocabulary of champs?

CAN'T!

Break the number one rule in our house, and it's grounds for having your mouth washed out with soap.

Even though it's not an official curse word. In the Shumake family, it might as well be, because it's the most destructive four-letter word I know.

In fact, when my children hear someone else say this word, they let out a chorus of

"Ooooohh!" in a way that says, "You're gonna get in trouble!"

And they'll call you out about it, too. Whether it's Grandma or a friend or a classmate, they will immediately correct you.

My kids know, that in order to be their best, they have to banish this dirty four letter word from their minds and mouths.

Can't kills ideas, spirits and visions. Can't poisons minds, deals and relationships. Can't blocks prosperity, productivity and passion.

So erase it from your conscience.

Forget that it exists. (Except when you hear someone else say it -- share the Language of Success with them!)

While you're focusing on CAN, think about the way you speak in general.

Learn to cast ideas and plans in a positive way. Successful people will tell you that they "speak" great things into existence.

For example, I don't say, "IF I raise a million dollars for The Robert S. Shumake Relays, I'll help people around the world." Instead, I say, "WHEN I raise a million dollars..." Likewise, I don't say "IF I buy my tropical paradise, I'll call it Refresher Island." Instead, I say with confidence: "WHEN I buy Refresher Island..."

And I don't walk around saying, "Oh, I hope I can do this deal."

No, I speak it in the affirmative, as if it's already happened: "This hot new deal is allowing me to expand my business in phenomenal ways."

On top of this, I say powerful words out loud that trigger me to take action. My favorite one is: "Execute! Execute! Execute!" That launches me into turbodrive.

I also come up with positive ways to express things that most people cast in the negative.

Rather than saying, "I'm having a difficult time meeting all the demands of my growing business," I say instead: "I have to stretch myself to succeed at all the exciting aspects of my booming business."

You see? I use the term "stretch" because it reminds me that I'm growing, expanding, getting bigger in every way.

I have a female friend who deals with any adversity -- especially if she's being criticized or rejected -- by repeating "Queen" over and over in her mind.

For her, whether it's her personal or professional life, she reminds herself that she's a queen and whatever outer forces are trying to bring her down, she's just not hearin' it.

When the autopilot of her mind flips into Queen mode, she literally lifts her chin with pride to deflect the negative vibes.

Another buddy of mine repeats from that beloved childhood book, "The Little Engine That Could." When fear and doubt choke his confidence, my friend whispers to himself, "I think I can, I think I can." And just like the little engine chugging up the hill with the heavy load of goodies, my buddy chugs through presentations, challenging projects and sticky situations. And he wins! Because he told himself, "I can." What words can you tell yourself -- during meetings or planning or working -- that will reroute your thoughts and actions onto a more positive path?

How can you change the way you talk to remove negative words and phrases, and replace them with uplifting, encouraging sayings and sentences?

Think about the incredible power of our words. Phrases like, "I love you" can inspire a person to do superhuman feats. But sayings like, "I hope you rot in hell," can downright destroy a person.

So own your words. Appreciate that each little letter you speak has the power to plant seeds of peace and prosperity in people and the world.

You can language your way to the top by simply speaking a new way to yourself and to others.

Folks who work with affirmations will tell you, the most powerful way to change your life is to reprogram your brain.

And you do that with the Language of Success.

Say it now: "I will! I shall! I can!
I CAN!"

WHY I CAN'T GIVE UP

"For one loss, all lost – the chain that held them would save all or none."

– Toni Morrison, Beloved

"A family working toward the same goal is worth more than a pot of gold."

– Robert S. Shumake

I CAN'T GIVE UP BECAUSE...

My momma didn't birth no loser.
My daddy didn't train no quitter.
My brother didn't hang out with no whiner.
My sister won't play with no failure.

My grandma don't take care of no disaster.
My grandpa won't listen to a half talker.
My aunts never gave room to low achievement.
My uncles hated to hear excuses.
My cousins wouldn't look at short vision.

My family wouldn't let me give up.
But, even if they did, I can't give up...
Because my momma, daddy, brother,
sister, aunts, uncles, grandma, grandpa,
and all my cousins would beat me if I did.

C all it your dream team.
Your village.
Your inner circle.
Your business family.
Your support group.

As the captain of your destiny in entrepreneurSHIP, you need a crew that you can trust with your life.

And it's only when you unknowingly steer into the blinding rain, wind and waves of a squall — one that's usually not forecast — that you can assess the quality of your crew.

Because it's easy for them to bask in the sunshine on deck, standing by you when it's all smooth sailing.

It's when the terrifying storms hit that you'll see just who has your back, and who doesn't. Because as an entrepreneur, you need a circle of folks who will risk their own safety to pluck you from the hurricane. You need people who will know -- before you even call for help -- that a giant wave washed up out of the blue and sucked you into a choking swirl of debt, confusion and terror.

You need men and women who have the experience to toss you a life ring, reel you in, and teach you how to keep a firm stance on deck, with a confident grip on the steering wheel.
You need this "Don't Quit" Team to give you

strength to keep treading water when you're about to sink.

Because I've learned, the times when we feel most exhausted and hopeless, we're actually swimming just a few strokes away from the sunken treasure. It's ours for the taking, if we can just muster a few more ounces of energy, another gulp of faith, and an additional jolt of fortitude. And we get those three things from our crew.

A good crew will tirelessly continue rowing those oars to help you sail into the Port of Prosperity.

I speak from experience. Because it was during moments when I saw no way out of a problem, that I called on my advisors. In a matter of minutes, they had the vision and good will to offer simple solutions to what I had viewed as overwhelming problems.

I realized, I have an entire village of entrepreneurs who are not only cheering me on, but they're counting on me to succeed.

Because when I win, so do they. By aligning with me and my mission, they are investing time, energy, money, wisdom and immeasurable gifts of dedication.

Call it peer pressure, but knowing that as captain of my particular endeavor, I'm representing a whole crew of folks who would drown in sadness if I quit, keeps me a float.

And quitting is not even an option when this family of colleagues, friends and mentors is cheering me on.

I call them family because our blood pumps with the same passion to use our gifts to make the world a better place. That kinship enables us to share dreams and goals. These individuals help to give me strength in times of controversy, change, and tribulation.

The best runner sprints even faster when folks on the sidelines are shouting for him to win.

The best captain of an entrepreneurSHIP invests the time and vision to assemble a super-star "Don't Quit!" crew.

*Identify individuals
who share your
vision and dreams.*

_____
_____
_____
_____
_____
_____

*Forge personal
relationships with
those in various
organizations
that can help you
succeed in business.*

_____
_____
_____
_____
_____
_____
_____

*List organizations
you can become part
of.*

_____
_____
_____
_____

SURVIVAL SKILLS

FOR

PERSEVERING

ENTREPRENEURS

SURVIVAL SKILLS FOR
PERSEVERING ENTREPRENEURS

Communicate that your business is one that solves problems, builds dreams, and provides answers.

Visualize how this is happening with each of your clients.

Learn about your market by going to trade shows, professional meetings, and by subscribing to trade publications.

Do market studies to find out what is needed: new products and/or improved services.

Don't assume that what you like is what everyone else likes and wants.

Set up a focus group and get feedback about your product or service including your pricing structure.

Send out an easy-to-complete survey to find out if your product is what is wanted.

Analyze these findings to determine how to change your product.

Learn about business through experience or extensive research, preferably both.

Be willing to work longer hours than on a regular job, especially during the first few years.

The average number of weekly working hours of a successful business person is 70.

PART FIVE

FUNDING AND RESOURCE DIRECTORY

* This is a directory of possible funding sources compiled. The author nor the publisher makes any guarantee of these sources as to contact information, integrity, or present availability. Seek each of them with business acumen by checking out any information received through proper sources (i.e lawyers, accountants, etc.)

PERSONAL LOANS

ALLIED INSURANCE
P.O. BOX 153686
Irving, TX 75015
(214) 255-4666
Consumer Loans
(Offices Nationwide)

AMERICAN GENERAL
FINANCIAL
27 South Stapley
Mesa, AZ 85204
(Arizona Only)

AVCO FINANCIAL
SERVICES
245 MAPLE ST.
Manchester, NH 03103
Consumer Loans in
NH & VT
Offices Nationwide

AVCO FINANCIAL
SERVICES
2278 East Lincoln
Anaheim, CA 92806
(714) 535-22-47
Consumer Loans
(California Only)

AVCO FINANCIAL
SERVICES
370 South Chambers Rd.
Aurora, CO 80017
(303) 745-9500
Consumer Loans
(Colorado Only)

COMMERCIAL CREDIT
CORP.
300 St. Paul Place
Baltimore, MD 21202
(Maryland and DC only)
Offices Nationwide

HEBREW FREE LOAN
SOCIETY
205 East 42nd St., Ste. 1318
New York, NY 10017
Borrowers must have two (2)
Guarantors from New York
area.

NATIONWIDE
FUNDING, INC.
3435 North Cicero
Chicago, IL 60641
(312) 777-7600
Personal Loans & Auto Loans
$1,000 - $10,000
Chicago area only

BUSINESS - REAL ESTATE AND SPECIAL SITUATION LOANS

ADVANTAGE FUNDING
1000 Parkwood Circle,
#300
Atlanta, GA 30339
800-241-2274
Accts. Receivables &
Factoring

AT & T CAPITAL CORP.
14 Southall Landings,
Ste. 100
Hampton, VA 23664
804-850-2698
SBA Loans $100,000 -
$1,200,000
For business & owner occupied
real estate. This office covers
VA & WV. for branch office
call 1-800-221-7275

ALLSTATE FINANCIAL
CORP.
2700 S. Quincy St., Ste. 540
Arlington, VA 22206
(703) 931-2274
Factoring for: Medical
Receivables, Government &
Service and Insured Receiv-
ables.

ANCHOR FINANCE
6310 San Vicente Blvd.,
Ste. 505
Los Angeles, CA 90048
(213) 932-1188
Secured Business Loans from
$50,000 up in SO. California,
NO RETAIL
OR AGRICULTURE

BANKAMERICA
BUSINESS CREDIT
10124 Old Grove Rd.
San Diego, CA 02131
(619) 549-7558

BEAN FACTORING
1333 Lawrence Expwy,
Ste. 218
Santa Clara, CA 95051
(800) 554-6992
Financing & Factoring
$15,000 up., CA only

BLACKBURNE & BROWN
MTG. CO.
4811 Chippendale Dr.,
Ste. 101
Sacramento, CA 95841
(916) 338-3232
First Morgages for Apart-
ments, Malls, Offices, Mobile
Home Parks & Strip Retail,
$50,000 - $750,000
CA only

BANKERS CAPITAL
4201 Lake-Cook Rd.
Northbrook, IL 60062
(800) 477-2000
Equipment Loans from
$5,000 up. Nationwide.

BANK AMERICA
BUSINESS CREDIT
40 East 52ND St.
New York, NY 10022
(212) 836-5210
All types of Business Loans
NO REAL ESTATE.
1 Million & up

CHURCH LOANS &
INVESTMENTS
P.O. Box 8203
Amarillo, TX 79114
(806) 358-3666
Church Loans Only
$100,000 - 2 Million
Call First

CIT GROUP/CREDIT FI-
NANCE
1235 West 30th St., 2nd
Floor
New York, NY 10020
800-245-0506 /
212-408-6124
All types of secured
Business Loans from 2 Mil-
lion up.

Branch Office & Phone No.
Los Angeles, CA
213-621-8500
Chicago, IL
312-424-9700
Dallas, TX
214-580-2600
The Texas Office lends in the
following states: AR, CO, LA,
MS, NM, OK and TX

CALIFORNIA FACTORS
& FINANCE
1609 West Magnolia Blvd.
Burbank, CA 91506
(818) 842-4891
Equipment & Account Receiv-
ables Financing. West Coast
Only.

CAPITAL FACTOS INC.
1799 W. Oakland Park Blvd.
Ft. Lauderdale, FL 33311
(305) 730-2900
Factoring from $100,000 up.

CAPITAL
INVESTMENT INC.
1009 W. Glen Oaks Lane,
Ste. 103
Mequon, WI 53092
(414) 241-0303
Business Loans $150,000 up
for Manufacturing & Services.
NO START-UPS.
Wisconsin Only

CASH FLOW
MANAGEMENT
P.O. Box 381119
Duncanville, TX 75138
(510) 537-7920
Factoring $20,000 up. TX only.
No Construction or Medical
Receivables

CERTIFIED
FINANCE, INC.
2021 Patio Dr., Ste. 215
Castro Valley, CA 94546
(510) 537-7920
Accounts Receivable
Financing. No Factoring,
California Only.

CITY LEASING
2001 Market St.
San Francisco, CA 94114
(415) 861-6000
Auto & Truck Leasing
Fleet Leasing to established
businesses, $5,000 up.
California Only.

COLONIAL MORTGAGE
& INVESTMENT
1201 S. Alma School,
Ste. 4950
Mesa, AZ 85210
(602) 703-1774
Real Estate Loans.
Arizona Only

COMMERCIAL
FACTORS OF CHICAGO
150 S. Bloomingdale Rd.
Ste. 200
Bloomingdale, IL 60108
(800) 448-2274
Factoring of Receivables.
No Construction Receiv-
ables. $10,000 up.
Nationwide & Canada

CONCORD
ACCEPTANCE CORP.
P.O. Box 3157
Rancho Santa Fe, CA 92067
(619) 759-0214
Construction Permanent &
Interim
Financing for Churches
Only.
$50,000 - 10 Million
35 States Nationwide

CONCORD
GROWTH CORP.
1170 East Meadow Dr.
Palo Alto, CA 94303
(415) 493-0921
Accounts Receivable Financing & Factoring. **No Medical or Construction Receivables** $50,000 up. West
Coast Only.

CONGRESS FINANCIAL
CORP.
1133 Ave. of the Americas
New York, NY 10036
(212) 840-2000
Asset Based Loans $3 Mil.
- $150 Mil. for buyouts,
turnaround financing,
equipment, bridge loans,
inventory, revolving term,
receivables, etc.

**CONGRESS FINANCIAL
Branch Office & Phone No.**

155

Pasadena, CA
(818) 304-4900
Miami, FL.
305-371-6671
Atlanta, GA
(404) 956-0094
Chicago, IL
(312) 332-0420
Boston, MA
(617) 338-1998
Baltimore, MD
(410) 997-1124
Portland, OR
(503) 227-7313
San Juan, PR
(809) 754-6560
Dallas, TX
(214) 761-9044

CUSHMAN CAPITAL
 MORTGAGE CORP.
2551 San Ramon Valley Blvd.,
Ste. 217
San Ramon, CA 94583
(510) 838-8130
Commercial Mortgages
$100,000 up. Northern California Only

DEUTSCHE
FINANCIAL SERVICES
2859 Paces Ferry Rd.
Ste. 1105
Atlanta, GA 30339
(800) 999-5733
Inventory & Receivables
Financing States: AL, GA, NC &
SC only
$25,000 up.

DNB
200 Park Avenue
Atlanta, GA 30339
(212) 681-3800
Debt Financing against Producing Oil Reserves or Oil &
Gas services
including offshore
5 Mil. up.

DRAPER & KRAMER, INC.
33 West Monroe
Chicago, IL 60603
(312) 346-8600
Commercial Loans for Income
Properties such as: Shopping
Centers, Office Bldgs, etc. 5
Mil. up. Nationwide

EMERGENT BUSINESS
 CAPITAL
15 S. Main St., Ste. 750
Greenville, S.C. 29606
(803) 232-6197
SBA Loans for owner occupied Commercial Properties
& Business
Loans $75,000 - 1 Mil. States:
DC, FL, GA, MD, NC,SC, VA.

EQUITABLE REAL
ESTATE
1150 Lake Hearn Dr.
#400
Atlanta, GA 30342
(404) 848-8724
Commercial Real Estate Loans
from 5 Mil.
Nationwide

FSFG LEASING CORP.
710 W. San Bernardino

156

Covina, CA 91722
General Lease Financing
to Start-Up Companies
$10,000 - $100,000.
Nationwide

FEDERAL NATIONAL
PAYABLES
7315 Wisconsin Ave.,
Ste. 322 E
Bethesda, MD 20814
(301) 961-6450
Factoring of Govt
Receivables only.
$3,000 up. Nationwide

FIRST CAPITAL CORP.
3503 NW 63rd St. Ste. 600
Oklahoma City, OK 73116
(405) 842-1010
Assets based Loans, Inventory, Accounts Receivable, etc.
$25,000 - 1 Mil.
Oklahoma & SW
Branch Offices & Phone No.
Westmont, IL
(708) 850-7876
Towson, MD
(410) 321-7966
Cleveland, OH
(216) 891-8888

FIRST FACTORS CORP.
P.O. Box 2730
High Point, NC 27261
(910) 889-2929
Factoring of Accounts Receivables from $100,000 up.
Nationwide. **No Medical or Construction Receivables**

FIRST FAMILY
FINANCIAL SVCS.
4362 Peachtree Rd. NE
Atlanta, GA 30319
(404) 266-5463
Residential Mortgages
Refinancing, Home Equity Loans. South Only.

FIRST SBIC OF
ALABAMA
16 Midtown Park East
Mobile, AL 36606
(205) 476-0700
Loans & Equity
Investments Up to
$500,000 Alabama Only

FLEET MORTGAGE
CORP.
50 Briarhollow,
Ste. 210 W
Houston, TX 77027
(800) 877-3049
Residential Mortgages &
Refinancing Texas Only
Nationwide

FOOTHILL CAPITAL
11111 Santa Monica
Blvd., Ste. 1500
Los Angeles, CA 90025
(313) 478-8383
Business Loans 1 Mil.
up for Asset based
loans, inventory, accts.
receivables, credit lines,
buyout/acquisitions etc.
Out of State 4 Mil. min.

157

FIDELITY FUNDING
275 East Baker St. Ste. A
Costa Mesa, CA 92620
(714) 437-5600
Factoring of Accounts
Receivables from $100,000
up. No Construction or
Medical Receivables. Na-
tionwide and Mexico

FINOVA CAPITAL
201 N. Figuerosa St.,
Ste. 900
Los Angeles, CA 90012
(213) 580-5610
Inventory, Receivables
Financing, Machinery &
Equipment Loans. Buy-
outs/Acquisition Loans
1 Mil. up. Nationwide

FREMONT FINANCIAL
CORP.
303 West Madison St.,
Ste. 500
Chicago, IL 60606
(312) 346-7676
Asset based loans, LBO's,
Turnaround Financing,
Lines of credit, Short term
loans, equipment & inven-
tory, factoring accounts
receivables loans. 1 Mil. up
Nationwide
Branch Offices & Phone No.
Santa Monica, CA
(310) 315-5500
Atlanta, GA
(404) 393-8400
Richmond, VA
(804)346-4122

GARBARK GROUP
3708 Woodrow St.
Brentwood, PA 15227
(412) 881-9299
Equipment Leasing from
$2,000 to 1 Mil for Print-
ing Co., Dry Cleaners,
Computers, Medical,
Commercial Trucking, etc.
Nationwide

GE CAPITAL
Small Business Finance
635 Maryville Center Dr.,
Ste. 120
St. Louis, MO 63141
(800) 477-2025
SBA Lender for all types
of Secured Business
& Commercial Loans
$100,000 up. NO Con-
struction or Apartments.
Nationwide

GE CAPITAL
260 Long Ridge Rd.
Stanford, CT 06927
800-243-2222
Mexico 011-52-5-228-9710
All types of Secured Business & Commercial Loans
$100,000 up
No Construction or Apart-
ments. Nationwide

GE CAPITAL
Commercial Finance
105 W. Madison, Ste. 1600
Chicago, IL 60602
(312) 419-0985
Asset based loans from 5
Mil. up; Leasing $100,000

up Nationwide

GLOBAL FINANCIAL
SERVICES
150 EAST 58th St.
New York, NY 10155
(212) 935-4370
equipment leasing $10,000
up. Acct's. Receivable &
Factoring
Sale/Leasebacks $150,000
up

GLOBAL
ACCEPTANCE CORP.
2004 Hogback Rd., Ste. 4
Ann Arbor, MI 48105
(313) 971-0985
Acct's. Receivable Loans
$10,000 up. Will handle
Construction Receivables

GOODMAN FACTORS,
INC.
3001 L.B.J. Freeway
Dallas, TX 75234
(214) 241-3297
Factoring of Accounts
Receivables; No Con-
struction or Medial Accts.
$10,000 up Nationwide.

HOME BENEFICIAL
LIFE INS.
3901 West Broad St.
Richmond, VA 23230
(804) 358-8431
First Mortgages for income

producing properties. States:
DE,DC, MD, NC,TN,VA,WV
$250,000 up

HEALTH CARE REIT
1 Seagate, Ste. 1950
Toledo, OH 43604
(419) 247-2800
1st Morgages, Sale/Lease-
backs. nursing Homes &
Pyschiatric Clinics. 2.5 Mil.
up Midwest & Southeast
Only

HELLER FINANCIAL
INC., 500 West Monroe
Chicago, IL 60661
(312) 441-7000
All types of business loans
& commercial real estate
loans. 5 Mil. up. Offices
Nationwide

HELLER FINANCIAL
SERVICES
101 Park Avenue
New York, NY 10178
(212) 880-7000
Business & Real Estate
loans 1 Mil. up Nationwide

HELLER
INTERNATIONAL CORP.
(Address & Phone the
same)
Specializing in the financing of international loan
projects.

INVEST AMERICA
CAPITAL CORP.
600 E. Mason St.
Milwaukee, WI 53202
(414) 276-3839
Secured Business/Equity
Investments $750,000 up.
Prefer Midwest

JEFFERSON PILOT LIFE
INS. CO.
100 N. Greene St.
Greensboro, NC 27401
(910) 691-3000
Loans for income produc-
ing projects. No Northeast
States. NO Apartments. 1
Mil. up.

LEXINGTON CAPITAL
CORP., 420 Lake Cook Rd.,
Ste. 114
Deerfield, IL 60015
(708) 374-1040 (Midwest
Only) Equipment Leasing
& Factoring of Accounts
Receivables. No Restaurant
Equipment, $10,000 up

LIBERTY LIFE
INSURANCE
P.O. Box 789
Greenville, SC 29602
(803) 268-8111
Commercial Real Estate
Loans. Industrial Office,
Retail w/Anchor. 1 Mil. up
Southeast Only.

LINC GROUP
303 East Wacker Drive
Chicago, IL 60601
(312) 946-1000 Nation-
wide Medical Equipment
will handle both venture
leasing & regular leases
$250,000 up

MICHIGAN CAPITAL
FINANCING, LTD.
2242 East Maple Avenue
Flint, MI 48507
(810)743-2322
All types of Equipment
Leasing. Specializing in
Medical Equipment & Sale
Leasebacks. No Rolling
Stock. $5,000 up. Nation-
wide

MONUMENT
MORTGAGE INC.
3021 Citrus Circle,
Ste. 150
Walnut Creek, CA 94598
(800) 322-9190
Residential Mortgages. CA
Only

NATIONAL
FACTORING SERVICES
1600 Stout St., Ste. 1050
Denver, CO 80202
(800) 253-6700
(303) 592-1919
City, State & Federal Gov't
Invoice Funding Nation-
wide

NATIONS FINANCIAL
CAPITAL CORP.
1 Canterberry Green
Stanford, CT 06901
(203) 352-4000
Commercial Mortgages,
Corporate Aircraft Financ-
ing, Barges & Vessels Fi-
nancing, Drilling & Quarry
Equipment, Railroad &
Helicopters, Buyouts Acqui-
sitions, Asset based loans 2
mil. up.
Nationwide

NORTHEASTERN
 LEASING
450 E. River Rd.
Grand Island, NY 14072
(716) 773-2044
Equipment Leasing. NY &
PA Only

MARWIT CAPITAL CORP.
180 Newport Center Dr.,
#200
Newport Beach, CA 92660
(714) 640-6234
Secured business loans from
$250,000, 4 Mil. NO Retail
or Start-ups. Nationwide

MASS TECHNOLOGY
DEVELOPMENT
148 State Street, 9th Floor
Boston, MA 02109
(617) 723-4920
Start up capital for techno-
logical companies in Mas-
sachusetts
$100,000. up

MEDITRUST
197 First Avenue
Needham Heights, MA
02194
(617) 433-6000
1st Mortgages, Construc-
tion Takeout for Health-
care Facilities Only. 5 Mil.
up

METRO FACTORS
P.O. Box 38604
Dallas, TX 75238
(800) 327-2274
Factoring $100,000 up
Nationwide

NYBDC CAPITAL CORP.
41 State Street
Albany, NY 12207
(518) 463-2268
Business & Commercial
Loans
New York Only $50,000
- $500,000

OXFORD FINANCIAL
7300 Old York Rd.
Philadelphia, PA 19126
(215) 782-7000
Factoring of Medical
receivables, Mobile Home
receivables, Time Shares.
1 Mil. up Nationwide &
Canada

161

ROSENTHAL &
ROSENTHAL
1370 Broadway
New York, NY 10036
(212) 356-1400
Factoring. Nationwide &
International $250,000
up

SHAWMUT CAPITAL
CORP.
200 Glastonbury Blvd.
Glastonbury, CT 06033
(203) 659-3200
All types of asset based
business loans 3 Mil. up
No Construction loans.
Nationwide
**Branch Offices & Phone
No.**
Sherman Oaks, CA
(818) 382-4267
Atlanta, GA 404-859-2400
Chicago, IL 312-346-8370
Boston, MA 617-742-9840
New York, NY 212-756-
7791
Dallas, TX 214-828-6500

RECEIVABLE FUNDING
CORP.
90 Park Avenue
New York, NY 10016
212-984-0748
Factoring

METROPOLITAN
LIFE INS. CO.
7100 N. Financial Drive,
Ste. 105
Fresno, CA 93710
209-435-0206

Farm/Ranch loans. California
only. Financing of income producing properties $500,000 up.

PMC CAPITAL INC.
17290 Preston Rd., 3rd Floor
Dallas, TX 75252
214-380-0044
SBA Lender for Business loans
$75,000 up. Nationwide

PACIFIC MUTUAL
LIFE INS. CO
700 Newport Center Dr.
Newport Beach, CA 92660
(714) 760-4355
Mobile Home Park Loans
3 Mil. up Nationwide

PRESTIGE CAPITAL CORP.
2 Executive Drive
Ft. Lee, NJ 07024
(201) 944-4455
Factoring $100,000 up
NO Construction
Receivables

PURITAN FINANCE CORP.
55 West Monroe Street
Chicago, IL 60603
(312) 372-8833
Accts Receivables &
Equipment Loans
Chicago Area $100,000 up

REPUBLIC FACTORS
CORP.
452 5th Avenue
New York, NY 10018
(212) 525-5200
Accts. Receivables & Factor-
ing Import/Export. Letters of
Credit

RIVIERA FINANCE
25 Walnut Street
Wellesley, MA 02181
(617) 235-0996
Accounts Receivables
Financing

SOUTH ATLANTIC
CAPITAL CORP.
614 West Bay Street
Tampa, FL 33606
(813) 253-2500
Equity & Later Stage
Financing from $500,000 up
for
Established Businesses only.
Southeast & Texas Only

TRIAD FINANCIAL INC.
1750 S. Telegraph,
Ste. 103
Bloomfield Hills, MI 48302
(810) 253-0100
Factoring of Accounts Receiv-
ables $5,000 up. NO Medical
Receivables or Construction
Receivables.

TLC FUNDING CORP.
660 White Plains Rd.
Tarrytown, NY 28231
(914) 332-5200
Secured Business Loans in
the Retail & Service Industry
Only. $50,000 up. Northeast
Only.

TRANSPORTATION
FACTORING
P.O. Box 10391
Portland, OR 97209

(503) 226-3493
Factoring for Transporta-
tion & Trucking Industry
$10,000 up.
Nationwide

UNION LABOR LIFE
 INSURANCE
111 Massachusetts Av-
enue N.W.
Washington, DE 20001
(202) 682-8786
First Mortgages &
Permanent Financing
for offices, Strip-Retail
Malls, Industrial Medical
Offices & Apartments.
Nationwide 4 Mil. up

U.S. REAL ESTATE
SERVICES
125 Maiden Lane
New York, NY 10038
(212) 709-6062 First
Mortgages, Permanent
& Standby Financing for
Offices & Strip Retail.
No Apartments. Must be
credit anchored. 2 Mil.
up. Nationwide

U.S. TRUST COMPANY
40 Court Street
Boston, MA 02108
(617) 726-7102
Asset Based Loans,
Inventory, Acct. Receiv-
ables, Machinery/Equip-
ment loan. 1 Mil up.
New England Only.

163

UNITED CREDIT
CORP.
15 West 44th Street,
5th Floor
New York, NY 10016
(212) 843-0808
Asset based lending
& factoring of receiv-
ables. No Construc-
tion Receivables: Toys
or Jewelry Receiv-
ables. $10,000 up.
Nationwide

UNIVERSAL
HEALTH REALTY
TRUST
7 Piedmont Center,
Ste. 202
Atlanta, GA 30305
(404) 816-1936
Permanent Financing
for Hospitals, Medi-
cal Offices, Nursing
Homes & Retirement
Homes. $2.5 Mil. up.
Nationwide

USL CAPITAL RAIL
SERVICES, INC.
733 Front Street
San Francisco, CA
94111
(415) 627-9250
Lease Financing for
Rail Cars & Tank
Cars, $100,000 - 10
Mil. Nationwide

U.S. REAL ESTATE
733 Front St. #210
San Francisco, CA

94111
(415) 627-4404
Permanent Financing for
Apartments, Multi-Tenant
Offices, Medical Offices,
Regional Malls, Warehouse
& Strip Retail 5 Mil. up.
Nationwide

VENTANA LEASING
8880 Rio San Diego Dr.
Ste. 500
San Diego, CA 92108
(619) 291-2757
Equipment Leasing from
$2,000 to 3 Mil. California
only

U.S. VENTURE PART-
NERS
2180 Sand Hill Road,
Ste. 300
Menlo Park, CA 94025
(415) 854-9080
Start-up & Expansion
Financing for Communi-
cations, Retail, Medial &
Computer Related 1 Mil.
up. West Coast Only

VARILEASE
31831 Camino Capistrano,
Ste. 101
San Juan Capistrano, CA
92675
(214) 248-4900
Equipment Leasing from
$150,000 up. Nation-
wide. Prefer High-Tech
Equipment. No Restaurant
Equipment

VEGA CAPITAL CORP.
80 Business Park Drive,
#201
Armonk, NY 10504
(914) 273-1025
Secured business loans from
$100,000 - 5 Mil. will handle
states: CT,NJ & NY only.
NO start-ups.

VENTANA
INTERNATIONAL
18881 Von Karman Avenue,
Ste. 350
Irvine, CA 92715
(714) 476-2204
Business expansions loans
from $100,000 to 1 Mil.
Prefer West Coast but will
handle on a Nationwide
basis.

WASHINGTON MUTUAL
LIFE
1202 3rd Avenue
Seattle, WA 98101
(206) 461-2100
Permanent Financing &
First Mortgages for Mort-
gages for Apartments
and Mobile Home Parks
$250,000 - 2.5 Mil. States:
OF,WA, ID,OR only

WELLS FARGO REAL
ESTATE
111 Sutter Street, 9th Floor
San Francisco, CA 94163
(415) 396-6614
First Mortgages for Apart-

ments, Offices, Anchored
'Retail & Industrial/Ware-
house. No Construction
Loans. California Only.
$500,000 - 10 Mil.

WESTERN
TECHNOLOGY
INVESTMENT
2010 North 1st Street, Ste.
310
San Jose, CA 95131
(408) 436-8577
Seed & Venture Leas-
ing from $250,000 up.
Nationwide. No Retail
Industries

WESTGATE CORP.
84 Washington Street,
2nd Floor
Hoboken, NJ 07030
(201) 222-3200
Factoring Accounts
Receivables & Purchase
Order Financing. Prefer
Garment Industry. No
Medical or Construction
Rec'v. $40,000 up. Na-
tionwide

WINFIELD CAPTIAL
CORP.
237 Mamaroneck Avenue
White Plains, NY 10605
(914) 949-2600
Business loans from
$200,000 - 1 Mil. No
Start-ups. Northeast
Only.

WINSTON
FINANCIAL GROUP
1532 B Brookhollow
Dr.
Santa Ana, CA 92705
(714) 979-2100
Factoring of Accounts
Receivables Prefer Medical Receivables $5,000
up. Nationwide

WOODSIDE FUND
850 Woodside Drive
Woodside, CA 94062
(415) 368-5545
Financing for communications, computer related,
health services, medical
related, and electronics.
Some Start ups. Will not
consider Real Estate, Oil
& Gas or Entertainment
Loans. $150,000 to 1 Mil.
West Coast Only.

WORKING
CAPITAL (Craig Basil)
3637 Mt. Diablo Blvd. Ste.
312
Lafayette, CA 94549
(510) 283-4433
Factoring Financing
$25,000 up. Nationwide

WORKING
VENTURES
CANADIAN FUND
65 St. Clair Avenue
East,

9th Floor
Toronto, ONT.,Canada
M4T 2X3
(416) 929-7777
All types of Business Expansion Loans from $100,000
up. Also, buyout acquisitions. No Start ups, Real
Estate, Oil & Gas Loans.
Canada Only

WHIRLPOOL
FINANCIAL CORP.
25 Tri-State International, Ste.
200
Lincolnshire, IL 60069
(708) 405-8200
Aircraft Leasing Nationwide
from 10 Mil. to 25 Mil.

ZENITH
FINANCIAL CORP.
540 Madison Avenue
New York, NY 10022
(212) 826-2282
Accounts Receivables Financing & Factoring $250,000 up.
Northeast Only.

INDUSTRY PREFERENCES OF VENTURE CAPITAL SOURCES

COMMUNICATIONS
Cable TV/Radio
Data Communications
Satellite Communications
Telephone Related

COMPUTER RELATED
Computer & Mini-Computer
Computer Hardware
Computer Software

DISTRIBUTION
Consumer Products
Electronics Equipment
High Technology Products
Health/Medical Products
Industrial Products

INDUSTRIAL/MANUFACTURING
Automation Equipment
Chemicals & Plastics
Consumer Products
Food Products
Industrial Products
Machine Tools
Raw Materials Processing

MEDICAL
Clinical Laboratories
Drugs & Medicines
Health Care Products/Services
Medical Instruments

NATURAL RESOURCES
Agriculture
Fishing/Forestry Products
Hazardous Materials
Minerals
Oil & Gas
Pollution Control
Recycling
Specialty Raw Materials
Waste Management

RETAIL
Discount Store
Retail Stores & Franchises
Other Retail

SERVICES
Advertising/Business Services
Banks & Finance Companies
Computer Services
Consumer Services
Education
Specialty Consulting

TECHNOLOGY
Advanced Materials
Analytical Instruments
Biological Sciences
Chemicals/Plastics
Engineering
Genetic/Medical Technology
Integrated Circuitry
Optics & Lasers
Pollution Control
Technology Related Products

VENTURE CAPITAL OR RISK CAPITAL LENDERS & INVESTORS

LISTED BY STATES

ALABAMA
HICKORY VENTURE CAPITAL
200 West Ct. Square, Ste. 100
Huntsville, AL 35801
(205) 539-1931
Industry Preferences: None
Geographical Preferences:
South/Southeast/Southwest
Minimum Size of Investment:
$500,000 up

JEFFERSON CAPITAL
P.O. Box 370928
Birmingham, AL 35237
(205) 324-7709
Industry Preferences: Communications, Manufacturing,
Medical, New Technology, Service Related
Geographical Preferences: Southeast
Minimum Size of Investment: $500,000 up

ARIZONA
ARIZONA GROWTH PARTNERS
9449 North 90th Street, Ste. 200
Scottsdale, AZ 85258
(602) 661-6600
Industry Preferences: HIGH TECH
Geographical Preferences: Arizona & Rocky Mountains
Minimum Size of Investment: $500,000 up.

FIRST INTERSTATE EQUITY CORP.
100 W. Washington Street
Phoenix, AZ 85003
(602) 528-6647
Industry Preferences: None/No Start-ups
Prefer Later Stage Financing
Geographical Preferences: Arizona
Minimum Size of Investment: $100,000 up.

172

CALIFORNIA
ADVENT INTERNATIONAL
2180 Sand Hill Road, Ste. 420
Menlo Park, CA 94025
(415) 233-7500
Industry Preferences: None
Geographical Preferences: None & International
Minimum Size of Investment: 1 Million up

ASSET MANAGEMENT COMPANY
2275 East Bayshore Rd., Ste. 150
Palo Alto, CA 94303
(415) 494-7400
Industry Preferences: Bio-Tech & Computer Software
Geographical Preferences: West Coast
Minimum Size of Investment: $100,000 up

AVI - 1 First Street, Ste 12
Los Altos, CA 94022
(415) 949-9855
Industry Preferences: Computer Related Only
Geographical Preferences: Silicon Valley Area
Minimum Size of Investment: $100,000 up.

AVALON VENTURES
1020 Prospect Street, Ste. 405
La Jolla, CA 92037
Industry Preferences: Medical Related Only
Geographical Preferences: California
Minimum Size of Investment: $100,000 up

BANKAMERICA VENTURES
950 Tower Lane
Foster City, CA 94404
(415) 358-6000
Industry Preferences: NONE
Geographical Preferences: West Coast
Minimum Size of Investment: $300,000 up

CALIFORNIA
BLALACK & CO.
130 S. SAN RAFAEL
PASADENA, CA 91105
(818) 440-5982
Industry Preferences: None
Geographical Preferences: Southern California
Minimum Size of Investment: $500,000 up

BRENTWOOD ASSOCIATES
11150 Santa Monica Blvd. Ste. 1200
Los Angeles, CA 90025
(310) 477-6611
Industry Preferences: Computer, Electronics, Medical
Geographical Preferences: None
Minimum Size of Investment: $500,000 up

BRYAN & EDWARDS
600 Montgomery Street, 35th Floor
San Francisco, CA 94111
(415) 421-9990
Industry Preferences: None
Geographical Preferences: West Coast
Minimum Size of Investment: $150,000 up.

CHARTER VENTURE
525 University Avenue, Ste. 1500
Palo Alto, CA 94301
(415) 325-6953
Industry Preferences: Computer and Medical Related
Geographical Preferences: West Coast
Minimum Size of Investment: $100,000 up

CALIFORNIA
CROSSPOINT VENTURE PARTNERS
1 FIRST Street, Ste. 2
Los Altos, CA 94022
(415) 948-8300
Industry Preferences: None
Geographical Preferences: California
Minimum Size of Investment: $100,000 up

DRAPER ASSOCIATES
400 Seaport Court, Ste. 250
Redwood City, CA 94063
(415) 599-9000
Industry Preferences: None
Geographical Preferences: West Coast
Minimum Size of Investment: $100,000 up

DSV PARTNERS
620 Newport Center Drive, Ste. 990
Newport Beach,CA 92660
(714) 759-5657
Industry Preferences: None
Geographical Preferences: West Coast
Minimum Size of Investment: $500,000 up.

GRACE HORN VENTURES
20300 Stevens Creek Blvd., Ste 330
Cupertino, CA 95014
Industry Preferences: None
Geographical Preferences: West Coast
Minimum Size of Investment: $250,000 up

CALIFORNIA
CROSSPOINT VENTURE PARTNERS
1 FIRST Street, Ste. 2
Los Altos, CA 94022
(415) 948-8300
Industry Preferences: None
Geographical Preferences: California
Minimum Size of Investment: $100,000 up

DRAPER ASSOCIATES
400 Seaport Court, Ste. 250
Redwood City, CA 94063
(415) 599-9000
Industry Preferences: None
Geographical Preferences: West Coast
Minimum Size of Investment: $100,000 up

DSV PARTNERS
620 Newport Center Drive, Ste. 990
Newport Beach,CA 92660
(714) 759-5657
Industry Preferences: None
Geographical Preferences: West Coast
Minimum Size of Investment: $500,000 up.

GRACE HORN VENTURES
20300 Stevens Creek Blvd., Ste 330
Cupertino, CA 95014
Industry Preferences: None
Geographical Preferences: West Coast
Minimum Size of Investment: $250,000 up

HAMBRECHT & QUIST
1 Bush Street, 18th Floor
San Francisco, CA 94104
(415) 576-3300
Industry Preferences: None
Geographical Preferences: Southwest & West Coast
Minimum Size of Investment: $250,000 up

CALIFORNIA
KLEINER, PERKINS, CAUFIELD & BYERS
2750 Sand Hill Road
Menlo Park, CA 94025
(415) 233-2750
Industry Preferences: Communications, Computer Related Electronics, Industrial Products, Medical Technology
Geographical Preferences Southwest & West Coast
Minimum Size of Investment: $100,000 up

MAYFIELD FUND
2800 Sand Hill Road, Ste. 250
Menlo Park, CA 94025
(415) 854-5560
Industry Preferences: Computer Related, Environmental Related, Medical Related, High Tech Manufacturing
Geographical Preferences: West Coast
Minimum Size of Investment: $250,000 up

OPPORTUNITY CAPITAL CORP.
(MESBIC)
2201 Walnut Avenue, Ste. 210
Fremont, CA 94538
(510) 651-4412
Industry Preferences: Broadcasting & Manufacturing
Geographical Preferences: West Coast
Minimum Size of Investment: $300,000 up.

OSSCO VENTURES
1 First Street, Ste. 15
Los Altos, CA 94022
(415) 917-0800
Industry Preferences: None/ NO RETAIL
Geographical Preferences: Western US
Minimum Size of Investment: $100,000 up

CALIFORNIA
QUEST VENTURES II
555 CALIFORNIA Street, Ste. 2955
San Francisco, CA 94104
(415) 989-2020
Industry Preferences: None
Geographical Preferences: California
Minimum Size of Investment: $100,000 up

SPROUT GROUP
3000 Sand Hill Road, Ste. 270, Bldg. 4
Menlo Park, CA 94025
(415) 493-5600
Industry Preferences: None
Geographical Preferences: None
Minimum Size of Investment: $500,000 up

SUTTER HILL VENTURES
755 Page Mill Road, #A-200
Palo Alto, CA 94304
(415) 493-5600
Industry Preferences: None
Geographical Preferences: None
Minimum Size of Investment: $100,000 up.

WEISS PECK & GREER VENTURE
555 California street, Ste.. 4750
San Francisco, CA 94104
(415) 622-6864
Industry Preferences: None
Geographical Preferences: None
Minimum Size of Investment: $500,000 up

COLORADO

CENTENNIAL FUNDS
1999 Broadway, Ste. 2100
Denver, CO 80202
(303) 298-9066
Industry Preferences: None
Geographical Preferences: Midwest
Minimum Size of Investment: $500,000 up

COLORADO VENTURE MANAGEMENT
4845 Pearl East Circle, Ste. 300
Boulder, CO 80301
(303) 440-4055
Industry Preferences: None
Geographical Preferences: Colorado
Minimum Size of Investment: $50,000 - $500,000

COLUMBINE VENTURE FUND, INC.
540 S. Quebec Street, Ste. 270
Englewood, Co 80111
(303) 694-3222
Industry Preferences: None
Geographical Preferences: Rocky Mountains/West
Minimum Size of Investment: $100,000 up

CONNECTICUT

CANAAN PARTNERS
105 Rowayton Avenue
Rowayton, CT 06853
(203) 855-0400
Industry Preferences: None
Geographical Preferences: New England
Minimum Size of Investment: $250,000 - 2 Mil.

CONNECTICUT

CONSUMER VENTURE PARTNERS
3 Pickwick Plaza
Greenwich, CT 06830
(203) 629-8800
Industry Preferences: Consumer related - No Start-Ups
Geographical Preferences: Northeast
Minimum Size of Investment: $500,000 up

MARKETCORP VENTURE ASSOC.
285 Riverside Avenue
Westport, CT 06880
(203) 226-2413
Industry Preferences: None. Prefer computer related
Geographical Preferences: Northeast
Minimum Size of Investment: $250,000 up

OAK INVESTMENT PARTNERS
1 Gorham Island, 1st Floor
Westport, CT 06880
(203) 226-8346
Industry Preferences: Medical, communications, computer related electronics, franchisee retail.
Geographical Preferences: Nationwide
Minimum Size of Investment: $500,000 up

RFE INVESTMENT PARTNERS
36 Grove Street
New Canaan, CT 06840
(203) 966-2800
Industry Preferences: None
Geographical preferences: Northeast
Minimum Size of Investment: $500,000 up

VISTA VENTURES
36 Grove Street

New Canaan, CT 06840
Industry Preferences: None
Geographical Preferences: Northeast
Minimum Size of Investment: $500,000 up

DISTRICT OF COLOMBIA
ALLIED CAPITAL CORP.
1666 K Street, NW, Ste. 901
Washington, DC 20006
(202) 331-1112
Industry Preferences: None/No Start Ups.
Geographical Preferences: East Coast
Minimum Size of Investment: $200,000 up

BROADCAST CAPITAL FUND
(MESBIC)
1771 N. Street NW, Ste.. 420
Washington, DE 20037
(202) 429-5393
Industry Preferences: Radio Stations
Geographical Preferences: None
Minimum Size of Investment: $200,000 up

NCB DEVELOPMENT CORP.
1401 Eye Street, NW, Ste. 700
Washington, DC 20005
(202) 336-7680
Industry Preferences: Agricultural Co-ops
Distribution
Geographical Preferences: None
Minimum Size of Investment: $50,000 up

FLORIDA
FLORIDA CAPITAL VENTURES
100 West Kennedy, Ste. 880
Tampa, FL 33602
(813) 229-2294
Industry Preferences: No Startups. Communica-

tions, Computer Related, Manufacturing, Technology
Geographical Preferences: Southeast
Minimum Size of Investment: $250,000 up

PMC CAPITAL CORP.
4000 Hollywood Blvd., Ste. 4355
Hollywood, FL 33021
(305) 966-8868
Industry Preferences: None/ No Startups, No Restaurants
Geographical Preferences: None
Minimum Size of Investment: $100,000 up

SOUTH ATLANTIC VENTURES
614 West Bay Street, Ste. 200
Tampa, FL 33606
(813) 253-2500
Industry Preferences: None - No Startups
Geographical Preferences: South & Southeast
Minimum Size of Investment: $100,000 up.

GEORGIA
ADVANCED TECHNOLOGY DEVELOPMENT
1000 Abernathy Road, Ste. 1420
(404) 668-2333
Industry Preferences: High Tech, Auto Industry After Market
Geographical Preferences: None
Minimum Size of Investment: $250,000 up

HAWAII
BANCORP HAWAII SBIC
P.O. Box 2900
Honolulu, HI 96846
(808) 537-8012

182

Industry Preferences: None
Geographical Preferences: HAWAII
Minimum Size of Investment: $50,000 up

PACIFIC VENTURE CAPITAL
222 S. Vineyard Street
Honolulu, HI 96813
(808) 521-6502
Industry Preferences: NONE
Geographical Preferences: HAWAII
Minimum Size of Investment: $50,000 up

ILLINOIS
ALLSTATE VENTURE CAPITAL
3075 Sanders Road, SO Plaza
Suite G5D
Northbrook, IL 60062
(708) 402-5681
Industry Preferences: None
Geographical Preferences: None
Minimum Size of Investment: $500,000 up

CAPITAL HEALTH VENTURES
122 S. Michigan Avenue, Ste. 1320
Chicago, IL 60603
(312) 427-1227
Industry Preferences: Medical/Health Only
Geographical Preferences: None
Minimum Size of Investment: $500,000 up

CILCORP VENTURES
300 Hamilton Blvd., Ste. 300
Peoria, IL 61602
(309) 675-8838
Industry Preferences: Environment
Geographical Preferences: None
Minimum Size of Investment: $300,000 up

ESSEX VENTURE PARTNERS
190 South LaSalle Stree, Ste. 2800
Chicago, IL 60603
(312) 444-6040
Industry Preferences: Medical Related Only
Geographical Preferences: None
Minimum Size of Investment: $50,000 up

FRONTENAC VENTURE COMPANY
135 S. LaSalle Street, Ste. 3800
Chicago, IL 60604
(312) 368-0044
Industry Preferences: None
Geographical Preferences: None
Minimum Size of Investment: $500,000 up

HELLER EQUITY CAPITAL CORP.
500 W. Monroe Street, 16th Floor
Chicago, IL 60661
(312) 441-7200
Industry Preferences: None/ No Startups
Geographical Preferences: None
Minimum Size of Investment: $2 Mil up

THE NEIGHBORHOOD FUND
(MESBIC)
25 East Washington Blvd., #2015
Chicago, IL 60603
(312) 726-6084
Industry Preferences: None / No Startups
Geographical Preferences: Chicago. Some WI, IN
Minimum Size of Investment: $50,000 up

WILLIAM BLAIR VENTURES
222 West Adams street
Chicago, IL 60603
(312) 236-1600
Industry Preferences: None / NO STARTUPS
Geographical Preferences: None
Minimum Size of Investment: I Mil up

WIND POINT PARTNERS
676 N. Michigan Avenue, Ste. 3300
Chicago, IL 60611
(312) 649-4000
Industry Preferences: None
Geographical Preferences: Midwest
Minimum Size of Investment: $250,000 up

IOWA

EQUITY DYNAMICS
2116 Financial Center
Des Moines, IA 50309
Industry Preferences: None / No Retail
Geographical Preferences: Midwest
Minimum Size of Investment: $150,000 up

IOWA SEED CAPITAL
200 East Grand Avenue
Des Moines, IA 50309
(515) 242-4860
Industry Preferences: None
Geographical Preferences: IOWA ONLY
Minimum Size of Investment: $50,000 up

KENTUCKY
KENTUCKY HIGHLANDS INVESTMENT
P.O. Box 1738

London, KY 40743
(606) 864-5175
Industry Preferences: Computer Related Distribution, High-Tech, Manufacturing
Geographical Preferences: Eastern Kentucky only
Minimum Size of Investment: $50,000 up

LOUISIANA

PREMIER VENTURE CAPITAL
451 Florida Street
Baton Rouge, LA 70801
(504) 332-4421
Industry Preferences: None / No Real Estate
Geographical Preferences: None
Minimum Size of Investment: $500,000 up

MAINE
NORTH ATLANTIC VENTURE FUND
70 Center Street
Portland, ME 04101
(207) 772-4470
Industry Preferences: None / No Real Estate
Geographical Preferences: Maine, Vermont, New Hampshire
Minimum Size of Investment: $250,000 up

MARYLAND

ARETE VENTURES, INC.
6110 Executive Blvd., Ste. 1040
Rockville, MD 20852
Industry Preferences: Communications, Environmental Waste, Gas/Electric Utility Industry
Geographical Preferences: Nationwide & Canada
Minimum Size of Investment: $250,000 up

JUPITER NATIONAL, INC.
39 West Montgomery Avenue
Rockville, MD 20850
(301) 738-3939
Industry Preferences: None/No Startups, No Retail, No Restaurants
Geographical Preferences: Northeast/South
Minimum Size of Investment: $250,000 up

NEW ENTERPRISES ASSOCIATES
1119 St. Paul Street
Baltimore, MD 21202
(410) 244-0115
Industry Preferences: None. Prefer Information Industry, Medical & Health
Geographical Preferences: None
Minimum Size of Investment: $100,000 up

MASSACHUSETTS
BOSTON CAPITAL VENTURES
45 School Street
Boston, MA 02108
(617) 227-6550
Industry Preferences: None
Geographical Preferences: New England
Minimum Size of Investment: $250,000 up

BURR, EGA, DELEAGE & CO.
1 Post Office Square #1330
Boston, MA 02109
(617) 292-7717
Industry Preferences: None. Prefer High-Tech Media
Geographical Preferences: East Coast
Minimum Size of Investment: 1 Mil. up

187

CHARLES RIVER VENTURES
10 Post Office Square #1300
Boston, MA 02109
(617) 292-7717
Industry Preferences: None
Geographical Preferences: New England
Minimum Size of Investment: $500,000 up

$\mathscr{A}$BOUT $\mathscr{T}$HE $\mathscr{A}$UTHOR

DR. ROBERT S. SHUMAKE is the founder of Inheritance Investment Group, a Michigan based real estate investment and development firm. Dr. Shumake's vision is to expand housing opportunities for people dreaming the American dream of home ownership.

Dr. Shumake received a White House appointment to the Board of Directors for the Federal Home Loan Bank Board, the second largest bank in America with 700 billion in assets. As a director, Dr. Shumake presided over the Affordable Housing Committees in Michigan and Indiana. Dr. Shumake was also appointed by the governor of Michigan, as a member of the Board of Real Estate Brokers and Salespersons with responsibilities to regulate and license real estate professionals.

Dr. Shumake has written *For Entrepreneurs Who Considered Suicide When Business Got Tough!* for individuals looking to achieve their entrepreneurial and financial dreams. The book is a guide, based on Dr. Shumake's experiences as an entrepreneur, for building wealth. Packed with quotes and helpful advice, as well as interactive pages for recording your personal and professional goals, "For Entrepreneurs Who Considered Suicide When Business Got Tough!" is a must have resource for anyone on a journey to do business well.

Dr. Shumake also encourages youth to exceed through the Robert S. Shumake Scholarship Relays; The largest private high school track and field meet in Michigan.

A dynamic spokesperson, Dr. Shumake has moved audiences throughout America and abroad with his candid stories about life and business. Information to contact him for your next meeting can be found on the following page.

Dr. Shumake is available for speaking engagements and seminars at your business, organization, church or corporation.

Contact information:
www.robertshumake.com
www.shumakerelays.com
www.Taketheland.com
www.RealCheapHouse.com

To Order Books call: 800-431-1579
Proceeds from the sale of: For Entrepreneurs Who Considered Suicide When Business Got Tough! *help to fund The Robert S. Shumake Scholarship Relays.*

Other Titles:

101 Reasons You Should Take The Land™
with Dr. Robert S. Shumake

Flipping Keys with Robert S. Shumake

CD:
12 Ways to Buy A Home No Money Down